brilliant

speed reading

brilliant

speed reading

Whatever you need to read, however you want to read it – twice as quickly

Phil Chambers

Harlow, England • London • New York • Boston • San Francisco • Toronto • Sydney • Auckland • Singapore • Hong Kong
Tokyo • Seoul • Taipei • New Delhi • Cape Town • São Paulo • Mexico City • Madrid • Amsterdam • Munich • Paris • Milan

PEARSON EDUCATION LIMITED
Edinburgh Gate
Harlow CM20 2JE
United Kingdom
Tel: +44 (0)1279 623623
Web: www.pearson.com/uk

First published 2013 (print and electronic)

ISBN: 978-0-273-78635-1 (print)
       978-0-273-79457-8 (PDF)
       978-0-273-79458-5 (ePub)
       978-1-292-00560-7 (eText)

British Library Cataloguing-in-Publication Data
A catalogue record for the print edition is available from the British Library

Library of Congress Cataloging-in-Publication Data
A catalog record for the print edition is available from the Library of Congress

The publisher is grateful to St Claire Thornhill for permission to reproduce the example on page 116, and to Elaine Colliar for permission to use the SEAHORSE acronym on page 109, originally devised and published in *The Student Survival Guide*, ECPC Publications, 2008.

10 9 8 7 6 5 4 3 2 1
17 16 15 14 13

Cartoons drawn by Cactus Designs

Print edition typeset in Plantin Std 10/14pt by 3
Printed in Great Britain by Henry Ling Ltd., at the Dorset Press, Dorchester, Dorset

NOTE THAT ANY PAGE CROSS REFERENCES REFER TO THE PRINT EDITION

This text is dedicated to all those who have attended my courses on speed reading. You have inspired me with your achievements.

Contents

About the author

Phil Chambers is the reigning World Mind Mapping Champion, a six times Mind Sports Olympiad Medallist and Grandmaster of Mind Mapping.

He has been a Buzan Speed Reading, Memory and Mind Mapping Instructor since 1995, trained by Tony Buzan (originator of Mind Mapping). Phil now trains speed reading instructors in collaboration with Tony Buzan.

In addition to this, he is a Registered Accelerated Learning Trainer, a Practitioner of Neuro-Linguistic Programming (NLP) and a member of the Professional Speaking Association.

Phil has conducted speed reading courses for various organisations, including the European Central Bank, lecturers at the University of Warwick and South Bank University, London, and many others.

He is author/co-author of five books, including *101 Top Tips for Better Mind Maps*, *A Mind to do Business* and *The Student Survival Guide*. He has acted as a consultant on *Max Your Brain* and *Train Your Brain to be a Genius* and his Mind Maps feature heavily in Tony Buzan's *The Mind Map Book*, *Mind Maps for Business* and *Use Your Head*.

Phil is Chief Arbiter of the World Memory Sports Council and Scorer of the Mind Sports Olympiad Memory and Speed Reading events. He is a founder member of the Mind Sports

Council and won the Special Services to Memory award in 1996 and 2010.

You can contact Phil through his training company, Learning Technologies Ltd, at **www.learning-tech.co.uk**, which specialises in offering bespoke solutions enabling companies and individuals to overcome problems and achieve their goals.

Acknowledgements

Thank you to Samantha Jackson, Lucy Carter and everyone at Pearson for helping bring this book to fruition. I would also like to thank all my friends, colleagues and clients who have contributed to the book with case studies, insights and support. Terry Brock, Tony Bukhari, Tony Buzan, Barry Connor, Chris Griffiths, Florence Mackay, Dominic O'Brien, St Claire Thornhill and to all the delegates on previous speed reading courses not mentioned by name but whose experiences and performance have shaped my writing.

Foreword

nformation is becoming cheap. We can find out what we need to know when we need to know it. The problem facing us today is how to manage the amount of information that is continuously bombarding us in every area of our lives. Knowledge is no longer power. Not even the use of knowledge is power. We need something else. We need new skills.

We're moving from a knowledge economy in which information was 'king' to a new age – an age where the management and creation of new knowledge is key. Success no longer depends on what you know, but what you can create. Today's computers can replicate all sorts of logical and information processing tasks but they cannot reproduce the imaginative thought processes of the human brain. Thus, information and logic are cheap, creative thinking is priceless!

We need new skills to enter this new age. To be creative we must be able to absorb more information, since the more we know, the more we can combine the existing knowledge we have in different ways to create new neural pathways in our brains – leading to personal original thoughts.

The more we know, the more we can create!

How do we get this additional information? Easy – we train our brain to filter and absorb relevant information quickly and, more importantly, we make sure it remembers more of that information.

The leaders of the future know that innovation and creative thinking are mandatory in the new economy. They've gone from being 'desirable' competencies to 'essential' ones. Without a constant flow of new ideas, our career or business is condemned to the backwaters. Others will progress, while we remain at a standstill.

To be innovative, we need to solve problems and make decisions, and in order to do this well we need to be able to think clearly and use information objectively. It's impossible to make the 'perfect' decision but there are ways and means to increase your chances of finding the best possible solution or course of action.

I have known Phil Chambers for over a decade and I have personally seen the positive impact his teaching has had on students and audiences around the globe. If you want to be able to remember more of what you read, and better still, read faster than you thought possible, then *Brilliant Speed Reading* is for you.

Chris Griffiths
CEO, ThinkBuzan and author of Grasp the Solution

Introduction

 'I just got out of the hospital. I was in a speed-reading accident. I hit a bookmark.'

Steve Wright

You hold in your hands what is probably the most influential book on your reading since you opened *Janet and John, Dick and Jane* or whatever books you read as a young child. Can you think of any areas of life where you haven't significantly developed your skills beyond what you learnt at primary school? There must be very few but it is likely that reading is one of them. In the next 12 chapters I will help you to transform your reading. Learning to speed read can change your life, freeing up a huge amount of time as well as improving your comprehension, retention and hence your studies and career prospects. Many people suffer from reading anxiety and stress caused by information overload. This book will give you the tools to regain control of the information in your life.

What you will need

Before starting you will need a pen or pencil to write in the book. This is seen by many as sacrilege but it is important. If you are reading a friend's book or have borrowed this from a library you can write in pencil and rub it out when you have finished.

You will also need something to time yourself. This can be a stopwatch, a clock or watch with a second hand, or a mobile phone with a timer app. If you are using a mobile phone make sure you switch it to silent mode so that it won't ring and break your concentration whilst reading.

Working out your reading speed will require a bit of long division. If you aren't confident about doing this longhand you will need a calculator or another mobile app.

For Chapter 7 you will need a chopstick, knitting needle or other slender pointer. You don't need to find this right away but if you are going to a Chinese restaurant soon, ask them if you can keep your chopsticks.

There are several exercises that you will need to do with a friend or colleague. If you are reading this book on your own, on a train or plane for example, you can skip the exercises and carry on reading, but it is important that you go back and do them as soon as the opportunity arises. The exercises will allow you to experience what I will be describing at certain points in the book.

How to use this book

Most speed reading books include practice passages that you can read whilst timing yourself to assess your speed. A lot of readers skip these. This book is different. It is written so that you can monitor your speed using the text itself as the test. When told to do so, start your timer. Towards the end of the chapter you will be told to stop your timer. The number of words are listed and you can work out your speed as follows:

> Your stopwatch reading will be something like 10:24.63. This is 10 minutes 24 seconds and 63 hundredths of a second. We can forget the hundredths, as these will make negligible impact on your time.

To work out your speed in words per minute you have to convert the seconds into a decimal number of minutes. Divide 24 by 60 to give 0.4 so your total time is 10.4 minutes. Let's say the chapter was 2,444 words. Divide the number of words by the time: 2444 ÷ 10.4 = 235 words per minute.

Don't worry if this sounds complicated, I will guide you through the process when required.

At the end of each chapter there are questions, totalling 10 points, to test your comprehension, with answers in Appendix 1. Answer these and mark your answers. Multiply your score by 10 to give a percentage comprehension. Both scores can be recorded in the chart at the end of this Introduction so that you can track progress. If you got any of the questions wrong, look back over that chapter to find the bits you missed.

We will use the remainder of the Introduction to assess your current reading speed. Read comfortably, as if you were just reading for pleasure, relax and don't rush unnecessarily.

START YOUR TIMER NOW

Why is speed reading useful?

As I see it, there are three main reasons to learn to speed read.

First, if you find yourself drowning in information, one of the things we will explore in Chapter 1, then increasing your reading speed can help you keep pace with the information that bombards you everyday.

Secondly, if you spend less time reading you will have more time to do the things you enjoy. This could be spending time with your loved ones or pursuing your hobbies instead of staying late at the office. If you have to read an important book at the weekend, wouldn't you rather get through it in an hour and spend that afternoon playing tennis or golf?

Thirdly, you can read more in the same length of time. By reading more widely and extensively, you acquire greater breadth and depth of knowledge. Sir Francis Bacon said, 'Knowledge is power'. I would prefer to say knowledge allows you to make more informed decisions, gives you more choices and the more you know, the easier it is to assimilate new information.

Contrary to popular misconceptions speed reading is not a trade-off between speed and comprehension. With the right techniques you can read, comprehend and retain information in a fraction of the usual time.

Have you have seen the film *Limitless*? The main character, Eddie Mora (Bradley Cooper) takes a pill that dramatically increases his mental capacity and powers of perception. He is able to access everything he has ever seen or read. This is, of course, science fiction and is impossible to achieve through drugs in real life, at least at the moment. However, if you take in information in the correct way you will be able to bring it back to mind when required. Speed reading will take you some way towards this panacea.

What is speed reading?

It is easiest to explain with an analogy.

When asked what the secret of success was for the all-conquering British cycling team, the performance director Dave Brailsford said it was 'the aggregation of marginal gains'. The same is true of speed reading. There is no *one* secret to success but a number of techniques, each of which will boost your speed and, when used in combination, will give great increases in both speed and comprehension. Just as with cycling, or any endeavour, practice is the key. Sir Chris Hoy and Victoria Pendleton did not win gold medals simply because of the technology behind their bikes. They spent hundreds or thousands of hours training. Speed reading does not require quite so much dedication but nevertheless you will only make major improvements through persistent practice.

Sometimes you will make big strides, at other times you may hit a plateau. Do not be deterred if your speed occasionally goes down or stays the same. Speed reading is all about changing your habits. If you have been reading slowly for 20 or more years, it is very easy to slip back into that deeply engrained pattern. Be sure to apply the speed reading techniques that you learn in this book to as much material as you can. The more you use them the more natural the techniques become.

What will I learn from this book?

In Chapter 1 I will help you put your current reading speed into context and see how you compare with expert readers and those who need to read fast to earn their living. You will also gain a better understanding of common problems and the necessity for strategies to deal with the 'info glut' that almost everyone is faced with on a daily basis. Finally, you will be asked to think about your current beliefs and attitudes to reading.

The process of seeing and reading is more complex than you probably think. It includes very intricate optics, biochemical and electrical signals and information processing involving many areas in the brain.

Chapter 2 introduces a new definition of reading. In very broad terms, it can be broken down into seven steps, each of which is vital to acquiring and applying knowledge.

Chapter 3 makes a very simple observation on how the eyes move when reading and draws out some very revealing conclusions. Once you have identified the characteristics that lead to slow reading you can eradicate or reverse them and hence speed up. In this chapter I discuss four elements that slow down your reading and show how doing the opposite can immediately increase your speed.

If you prepare appropriately and learn how to get into a good state of mind you can improve your speed without applying additional physical reading techniques. Chapter 4 includes numerous techniques to improve motivation and manage your state of mind. This not only helps to make reading more enjoyable, it also tackles boredom and distractions.

Chapter 5 delves deeper into the science of vision, considering the use of both your central focus and your wider peripheral vision. Simply by changing the distance that you hold your book, you can improve the efficiency of your vision, reduce eye strain and fatigue, and improve both speed and comprehension.

Chapter 6 differs from the majority of the book by switching attention to techniques that involve trading comprehension for extreme speed. In this chapter I consider skimming, scanning and selective reading. These techniques help you to get an overview of a book before deciding whether to read it from cover to cover or find which bits are relevant. In some instances skimming or scanning can be enough to achieve your aims and so can save you a massive amount of time.

Chapter 7 introduces the concept of using a physical guide to assist your eyes in tracking across a page of text. Use of a guide, once mastered, is one of the most important techniques in speed reading. It supports the techniques described in Chapter 3 and gives you the means to directly control and manage your reading speed.

In Chapter 8 I turn my attention to comprehension and retention of information. Without these two factors speed is meaningless, but only through speed do you achieve them. Increased comprehension and speed go hand in hand. Slow reading leads to less focus, reduced comprehension and more confusion.

If you are a student at college, university or studying for professional exams, reading is a massive part of your life. To study effectively, reading is not enough. You need a strategy to manage your use of time, your note-taking and your retention of information. Chapter 9 introduces you to a range of powerful memory techniques and study skills to support your learning.

In the modern world we spend more and more time in front of computer screens. This has dangers in terms of the wellbeing of your eyes, often leading to myopia or other disorders. Computers also present a wealth of distractions from email to surfing the web. Despite the disadvantages there is a wealth of positive aspects to reading from a computer screen, not least the flexibility to alter text to suit your own preferences. Chapter 10 offers solutions to the problems and recommendations on how to adapt text based on research from NASA, Microsoft and others.

Although, as we will see, a limited vocabulary is not necessarily a barrier to reading fast, the wider your vocabulary the easier it will be to comprehend what you are reading. For those of us without a classical education, the prospect of learning new words can be daunting. In Chapter 11 I explain how, by learning the Latin and Greek building blocks of language, you can unlock the meanings of hundreds or even thousands of words.

Chapter 12 draws together the different themes in the book and reflects on what you have learnt. I summarise the key techniques, offer suggestions for the continued development of your reading skills and answer questions. I also consider the implications of speed reading on an often overlooked application – the alleviation of dyslexia.

I hope that you enjoy this book and gain valuable insights into what can ultimately be a life-changing skill. If you are to measure your improvement, try to read each chapter in one go rather than reading part of the way through and then coming back to it. If you are reading at about 200 words per minute then it will take about 15 minutes to read the text plus about 5 minutes to answer and mark the comprehension questions. Of course, as your speed increases, you will be able to get through the later chapters far faster.

STOP YOUR TIMER NOW (word count: 1,422)

Comprehension questions

(Points in [ ] brackets after each question)

1   Speed reading is a trade-off between speed and comprehension. True or False? [1]

2   How did Dave Brailsford describe the secret of success of the British cycling team? [1]

3   What is the key to making major improvements in reading speed? [1]

4   What single action can improve the efficiency of your vision, reduce eye strain and fatigue, and improve both speed and comprehension? [1]

5   Which two techniques help you to get an overview of a book before deciding whether to read it from cover to cover or find which bits are relevant? [2]

6   Use of what is described as one of the most important techniques in speed reading and gives you the means to directly control your reading speed? [1]

7   What advantage does reading from a computer screen have according to the text? [1]

8   Knowledge of which two languages helps you to build vocabulary? [2]

Check your answers in Appendix 1.

Number of points × 10 = % comprehension

Calculation

Timer reading

Minutes:

Seconds: divide by 60 and add to whole minutes

1,422/time =   Speed (words per minute)

Enter your comprehension and speed in the chart overleaf.

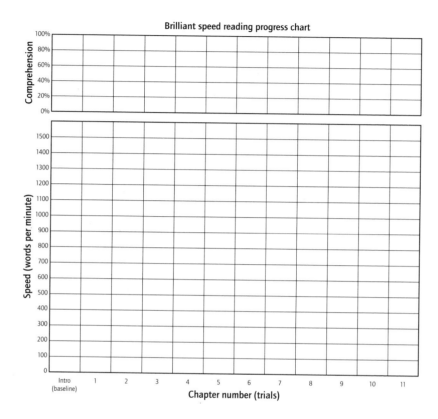

Brilliant speed reading progress chart

CHAPTER 1

Putting your reading speed into context

You should have a figure of your current reading speed in the first column of the record chart. If you skipped the Introduction, go back and read it before continuing.

In this chapter I aim to put your speed into context. You will see how you compare with the world record holder, presidents and professors. Don't let this intimidate you at the start of your journey. Over the course of this book you will see your speed build bit by bit as I introduce you to more components of the technique. Most very fast readers started off reading slowly.

I will also discuss how speed reading is an important part of a wider arsenal in the fight against the tyranny of information overload.

We will look at common problems that almost every group that I teach come up with and examine your beliefs about reading. This will serve as a useful comparison to Chapter 12 at the end of the book.

I will also offer some advice for increasing comprehension simply by putting in a little preparation before embarking on reading.

Information overload

We are living in a time of ever-increasing amounts of information. In 2010 Google counted what they consider to be every single book in the world, arriving at a staggering total of 129,864,880. A person living today receives more information in a single day than someone living in the seventeenth century received during the course of an entire lifetime.

Digital overload

The advent of the computer and the internet has hastened the pace of information generation. Google now estimates that there are over a trillion web pages. As of 2007, the world's information storage capacity was an estimated 295 exabytes. In the same year we broadcast nearly 1.9 zettabytes of data, equivalent to each person on the planet reading 174 newspapers daily (Hilbert and Lopez 2011; quoted in Griffiths and Costi 2011). With the democratisation of electronic publishing and broadcasting, anyone can be an author with an average of 58 million tweets on Twitter per day (**www.statisticbrain.com**) and 450 million English-speaking blogs.

Email has become ubiquitous, taking up a massive amount of time. Recently it was estimated that 247 billion email messages are sent per day worldwide, 81 per cent of which are spam. We need to break our addiction to Facebook and devices like BlackBerries, iPhones, etc that tie us to email and reading unnecessary messages. I know this is easier said than done. I was lost without my laptop when it had to go into repair in February 2012. I had no email and no web access. With my VAT return having to be filed online and my banking internet-based, I had to borrow an iPad to meet the deadlines and avoid a fine. It was a salutary lesson in just how technology-dependent life has become. In her highly thought-provoking 2003 book *Tomorrow's People*, Professor Susan Greenfield warns of the dangers to the mind and individuality resulting from new scientific advances and increasing interconnectedness.

'... Now we face a future of interactive and highly personalised information technology, an intrusive but invisible nanotechnology, not to mention a sophisticated and powerful biotechnology, that could all conspire together to challenge how we think, what kind of individuals we are, and even whether each of us stays an individual at all.'

Professor Susan Greenfield

Information overload in business

The majority of the world's corporate memory is stored in some sort of paper form. Having too much information is having devastating consequences on business and a typical enterprise spends between 3 and 5 per cent of its revenues managing documents. This cost is frequently higher than what they invest in research and development (Xerox internal study). Swamped by information, mistakes inevitably happen with 42 per cent of people accidentally using the wrong information at least once per week; 53 per cent believe less than half of the information they receive is valuable (Griffiths and Costi 2011).

How about you?

- How long do you spend reading and responding to email?
- Do you have a stack of unread newspapers and magazines?
- Do you have unread books on your bookshelf?
- Do you have boxes, drawers, files or stacks of reports, letters and other information all unread?

Almost everyone at one time or another feels overwhelmed with the glut of information bombarding us. We are drowning!

So what is the solution?

Technology has a role to play. Most email programs now have an automatic spam filtering function. Internet service providers can also install mail filters in their mail transfer agents as a service to all of their customers. This can't yet eradicate spam, with clever marketers finding ways to circumvent automated systems, though the technology is becoming more and more sophisticated. You can reduce the amount of reading required to find a relevant fact on the web by using intelligent internet search tools such as Wolfram Alpha, written by British scientist Stephen Wolfram. This is described as an 'answer engine' rather than a 'search engine'. Wolfram Alpha is capable of responding to particularly phrased, fact-based questions in natural English. The technology is still in its infancy but will undoubtedly develop.

Being selective in your reading is vital. You need to filter out the unnecessary information. You could ask, 'How do you know what is important until you have read it?' In Chapter 6 I will explain how to work with document structure to find where the important nuggets are located and use techniques such as skimming and scanning to get a précis before committing to reading in depth.

The final piece of the puzzle, once you have reduced the tsunami of information to a mere flood, is reading faster. So how fast is it possible to read and how do you compare to super speed readers?

Speeds across the population

The average reading speed is in the region of 200 to 240 words per minute (wpm) with about 60 to 80 per cent comprehension. This varies according to the difficulty of the text and the other factors such as tiredness, time of day, etc that we will discuss in later chapters. When studying and note-taking, speed can drop to under 90wpm. How does your current speed compare with this average? Don't worry if you scored less than 200wpm. With the techniques in this book you can easily double or triple your speed and, with practice, increase it even more.

Functional literacy

The term 'functional literacy' came into common use in the 1960s, when the United Nations Educational, Scientific and Cultural Organization (UNESCO) began addressing the lack of literacy skills among a large percentage of the population of adults and out-of-school children in developing countries. The term is used in different contexts but can be broadly defined as the level of skill needed to 'function fully in society and meet personal and social needs in general education'. The characteristics of functional literacy vary from one culture to another, as some cultures require better reading and writing skills than others. A reading level that might be sufficient to make a farmer functionally literate in a rural area of a developing country might not qualify as functional illiteracy in an urban area of a technologically advanced country. About 20 years ago UNESCO established a minimum reading rate they thought people needed to achieve in order to be functionally literate in developed countries of 400wpm. As already discussed, the pace of change has increased so rapidly that the 400wpm minimum speed is almost certainly out of date. A level of at least 600wpm may be more appropriate.

Super speed readers

In surveys of general reading speed, about 1 in 100 people read at between 800 and 1,000wpm. People in this range are usually in roles where they need to read extensively for their work. This includes top professors, researchers, politicians or editors. The figure falls to one in a thousand for individuals reading at speeds over 1,000wpm. The world record holder, former English teacher Anne Jones, was able to read *Harry Potter and the Deathly Hallows* in under 47 minutes immediately after it was realised at midnight on 21 July 2007. This equates to a rate of 4,251wpm. Her comprehension was sufficiently good to write a credible review of the book for the following day's newspapers and *Sky News*. To do this she had to familiarise herself with J.K. Rowling's literary style and spend time training, just as a physical athlete would in preparation for a major race. Despite this remarkable performance, Anne does not have a natural talent for reading. She just uses the techniques that I cover in this book and puts in a lot of practice.

Other individuals who have learnt to speed read with good effect include US Presidents John F. Kennedy and Jimmy Carter. Kennedy was a great proponent of speed reading. He reached speeds of around 1,000wpm after taking a speed reading course with his brother Bobby and encouraged many in his Cabinet to take similar courses. This helped make speed reading popular throughout the United States in the 1960s.

brilliant example

'There was a time when, as a software developer, I carried a single textbook around with me to ensure that I could address any technical issue I encountered. The book was *The C Programming Language* by Brian W. Kernighan and Dennis M. Ritchie and a knowledge of its contents ensured I could create computer programs for any of the hardware platforms available.

How things have changed! It seems that these days I am dealing with a new technology every week. This causes me to constantly read new publications dealing with the many facets of modern software development. So when I came across the concept of speed reading I looked into its claims and decided that although the claims were obviously exaggerated, even a modest improvement in my reading speed would be beneficial, so I enrolled in a course. During the course I was amazed that my reading speed improved from 148 words per minute to 1,000 words per minute! I used my new found ability to read a 4,000 page technical manual in an hour - which resulted in a new level of reading enjoyment coupled with enhanced comprehension of the content.'

Barry Connor, Founder of dotNet Specialists

It is important to remember that once you have mastered speed reading you can choose how fast you want to read. If you have a lot of material that you have to assimilate rapidly then speed reading will be the ideal technique. If, on the other hand, you go to bed with a book or e-reader and your aim is to relax, it would be more appropriate to read deliberately slowly. We will consider this idea of a range of reading speeds in more detail later (Chapter 12).

brilliant tip

Often the purpose of reading is to gather information. If you can get what you need without reading every word that is great. Take what you need from a text and move on.

Typical problems with reading

Having taught speed reading to many different nationalities, I hear similar problems are mentioned regardless of age, cultural background, gender or level of education. A typical selection of comments include:

Fear

● Faced with a large book I feel intimidated.
● If I speed up, I am frightened that I will be missing important points.

Overload

- The pace of technological changes is so fast that I can't keep up.

- Time is too short to read even a fraction of what I need to.

Frustration

- I am frustrated by the lack of progress made when reading.

- Reading feels like a chore or a punishment.

- I am frustrated and intolerant of books that don't get to the point. I resent having to read too much description before anything happens. Life's too short!

- When I proofread emails, I never notice the mistakes until after I click 'Send'.

- Why can I never spot errors in my own writing?

Guilt and social pressure

- There are too many books that I should read.

- I feel guilty that I am neglecting my family when I spend hours reading.

- We have been conditioned to always read a book from beginning to end, slowly and one word at a time.

- When you should read a book for work it becomes a burden. I have lots of books that I should read but I haven't and lots of books that I have read for pleasure that were easy to read fast.

Lack of focus

- I will often drift off into my imagination when reading.

- I am easily distracted.

- I get inspired by ideas in the book and my mind wanders.

- I start to daydream when I should be reading.

- I can't concentrate or focus for long.

- I don't finish books. With my iPad I can carry around many more books than I physically used to be able to. I end up reading several in parallel. I jump around and never finish any.

- I have to keep going back over text, sometimes four times.

Boredom

- If there aren't graphics, colour and nice fonts in a book I get bored.

- When I start to read, I feel tired and sleepy.

- When I open a book my heart sinks.

Can you relate to any of the above problems? Over the course of reading this book these challenges will all be addressed and eliminated.

Increasing comprehension through questioning

Research has shown that if you ask yourself questions before you study or read you will be more engaged and retain more information. Good teachers and lecturers ask their students to discuss and think about questions rather than simply give them the answers. The word 'educate' is directly derived from the Latin word 'educare'. The literal translation is 'to draw out of' or 'to lead out of'. The Romans considered educating to be synonymous with drawing knowledge out of somebody or leading them out of their usual thinking. This is closely related to the teaching of the Greek philosopher, Socrates. The Socratic Method employs a series of questions formulated as tests of logic and fact intended to help a person or group discover their beliefs about a given topic.

How do you do this in practice?

Obviously, if you are reading with a specific goal in mind, for example, researching information for an essay or a report, you should have well-defined questions and therefore be well-prepared for effective reading. This will not only direct your reading towards a goal, but also help to focus your attention. Try to raise questions that lead to more active reading. These could include:

- What clues does the title/subtitle reveal?
- What expectations do you have?
- What information do you know about this topic?
- Why are you reading this article?
- What information do you hope this article will include?
- What questions do you hope this article will answer?
- Do you know this author's work?
- Have you read other pieces written by this author?
- What do you know about the kinds of writing this author has composed?
- Why do you think the author wrote this article?

If your reading is more general, then you can employ Rudyard Kipling's *Six Honest Serving Men*:

> *I keep six honest serving-men*
>   *(They taught me all I knew);*
> *Their names are What and Why and When*
>   *And How and Where and Who.*
> *I send them over land and sea,*
>   *I send them east and west;*
> *But after they have worked for me,*
>   *I give them all a rest.*

I let them rest from nine till five,
For I am busy then,
As well as breakfast, lunch, and tea,
For they are hungry men.
But different folk have different views;
I know a person small–
She keeps ten million serving-men,
Who get no rest at all!

She sends 'em abroad on her own affairs,
From the second she opens her eyes –
One million Hows, two million Wheres,
And seven million Whys!

Rudyard Kipling
From 'The Elephant's Child' in *Just So Stories*

The six questions make a good starting point to tackle a book. Of course you need to adapt them to the particular situation. In a study book, 'what', 'why' and 'how' will probably be more important than the other three. These can be developed further to give more specific questions as follows:

Definition

What is … ?

Where does … fit?

What group does … belong to?

Characteristics

How would I describe … ?

What does … look like?

What are its parts?

Examples

What is a good example of ... ?

What are similar examples that share attributes but differ in some way?

Why did the author choose the examples they did?

Experience

What experience have I had with ... ?

What can I imagine about ... ?

When reading this book, if you like, you can read the Comprehension questions at the end of the chapter before reading the text. This may slightly skew the measure of comprehension, as you will be hunting for the answers in the text. If you are focused on getting the most out of the book, knowing the questions in advance will help. If, on the other hand, you want quantitative data on your improvement then it is best to read first and look at the questions afterwards.

STOP YOUR TIMER NOW (word count 2,911)

Comprehension questions

1 How many billion dollars in productivity does the US economy lose to information overload each year? [1]

2 Name two ways that technology can help reduce information overload. [2]

3 What is the average reading speed and comprehension? [2]

4 What speed did UNESCO declare as the minimum to be classed functionally literate? [1]

5 To the nearest thousand words per minute, how fast did Anne Jones read *Harry Potter and the Deathly Hallows*? [1]

6   Name two of the six main categories of problem
    mentioned. [2]

7   What can you do before reading to increase comprehension
    and retention? [1]

Check your answers in Appendix 1.

Number of points × 10 = % comprehension

Calculation
Timer reading
    Minutes:
    Seconds: divide by 60 and add to whole minutes

2,911/time =   Speed (words per minute)

Enter your comprehension and speed in the chart in the
Introduction.

 **exercise**

Your attitudes and preconceptions about reading

You probably don't often think about your attitudes and beliefs about
reading. Many of these attitudes originate from your schooling as a child.
Did you always simply take your teachers' word for it or do you have direct
evidence to back up your beliefs? This book will challenge some of those
beliefs. Complete the exercise below as a snapshot of your current thoughts
about the nature of reading.

Consider each of the statements overleaf. Place a tick in the left-hand
column if the statement is true, the middle column if you were taught this
in the past but now believe it is not true and the right-hand column if it is
false. Leave blank if you don't know.   ▶

	True	Taught	False
Don't subvocalise (say the words under your breath to yourself or hear the words in your head).			
Using your finger to point to words on a page is wrong. It slows you down and is childish.			
To understand a book's contents you must read it 'slowly and carefully'.			
Always start reading at the beginning of a book and go through to the end.			
Go back and understand what you are reading before you go forward.			
Each word must be read separately.			
As you read faster, your comprehension drops.			
Look up a word that you do not know right away.			
It isn't natural to read fast.			
You cannot appreciate the material if you read it fast.			
Motivation plays no role in reading speed.			
It is not necessary to rest or exercise your eyes.			
Comprehension should always be 100%.			
You cannot see any wider than a page.			
You can only read what you are directly focusing on visually.			
You must not mark or write in books.			
There is no relationship between reading and your belief system.			
Sit still until you have finished.			
If it is in print it is probably true.			
The brain's ability to shift and adapt to a situation has no role in reading.			

We will return to this list in Chapter 12.

CHAPTER 2

A definition of reading

START YOUR TIMER NOW

D
o you ever think about *how* you read?

When you pick up a book, newspaper or digital device and start to read, it probably just feels like you are absorbing information without thinking about the process. It has become an unconscious skill. However, when you pick apart the steps that go from seeing printed marks on a page or screen to forming a mental representation of the meaning, it is a very complex process.

Reading involves very intricate optics where the cornea and lens focus an upside-down image on the light-sensitive cells of the retina at the back of eye. Biochemical systems translate the image into electrical signals and information processing involving many areas in the brain translate this into an experience of 'seeing'. Of course, reading is far more than seeing and yet more areas of the brain decode language to form imagined sounds and pictures. This is not a neuroscience or anatomy textbook so I will largely ignore the mechanics of seeing words for the moment, though we will discuss this a little more later (Chapters 3 and 5).

In very broad terms, reading can be broken down into seven steps.

1 Recognition

Assuming you don't speak Mandarin, if I gave you a page of Chinese text you wouldn't be able to read it. The first step of reading is recognition of the characters that make up the text. As you're reading this book in English the characters are the Roman alphabet. These combine to form words and eventually sentences.

Do you remember how you were taught to read? There are two main methods. The one currently favoured by British government educational advisors is called Synthetic Phonics. This teaches the sounds associated with individual letters and combinations of letters in isolation. For example, children might be taught a short vowel sound (e.g. /a/) in addition to some consonant sounds (e.g. /c/, /t/). Then the children are taught to blend the sounds together to form the word (e.g. /c/ -/a/ -/t/; 'cat'). The alternative method is the Look–Say system where whole words are introduced with a verbal response. For example, the child is shown a picture of a cat with the word clearly printed underneath. The teacher asks the child to identify the word (and picture) verbally. If the child says 'doggie', for example, they are corrected before moving on to the next picture. Eventually, the pictures are removed, the child identifies just the words and is in a similar position to someone who is taught phonics.

Both methods have merit. Using synthetic phonics, children generally take less time to learn to read and they can tackle unfamiliar vocabulary more easily. Both methods involve saying the words out loud and hence virtually all readers still 'hear the words in their heads' when reading, a process called 'subvocalisation'. This is necessary for comprehension and some slow readers actually mouth the words or mumble them under their breath. Many teachers of speed reading advocate the total elimination of subvocalisation. In fact one online course claims, 'The point to be made is that as long as you continue the habit of subvocalisation, you will never achieve reading speeds associated with excellent readers which are 700 or more words per minute.' This is not my approach as subvocalisation has many benefits in terms of memory and comprehension. It need NOT slow you down, as we shall see (Chapter 8).

2 Assimilation

Having recognised the words of a piece of text, the next step is actually taking them in. Have you ever reached the bottom of a page when reading a book but with no idea about what you read? Your recognition of the words was fine but your assimilation was nearly zero. The process of assimilation relies on your eyes and brain working in harmony. There are many factors that influence assimilation. These include:

Your physical wellbeing

It is hard to read effectively if you are excessively tired. Illness will dramatically reduce your reading speed and comprehension.

If you are particularly physically unfit your reading will be less effective. Remember the Latin saying, '*Mens sana in corpore sano*' (a sound mind in a healthy body).

Your environment for reading

By far the easiest and quickest way for anybody to improve their reading concentration is to remove physical discomfort when reading.

Choose a comfortable chair with a straight back, neither too soft nor too hard. It should support your neck, shoulders and upper back so that you sit upright with good posture. Bad posture, with a hunched back and a compressed chest, leads to shallow breathing and reduces the amount of oxygen reaching the brain. It can also contribute to back pain and other related problems. Kneeling chairs are an option as they reduce lower back strain by dividing the burden of the weight on the shins as well as the buttocks and pelvis. A common problem is that people choose to read on a comfy sofa or sinking into an armchair, curled up or with their legs outstretched on a footstool. Some people even read whilst lying on their bed during the day. In all these cases you are far too relaxed to engage with the book and are just promoting sleep. It is advisable to read at a desk at a comfortable height.

When you sit in a chair for a long period of time, it is important that the blood circulation to your legs continues. You should sit so that your thighs are parallel to the floor when your lower legs are upright and your feet flat on the floor. In other words, the front of your seat should not cut off the blood supply to your legs. You can always use a little foot platform to lift up your feet and legs, if you need to have your seat higher when sitting at a desk, for example.

brilliant tip

Do not cross your legs whilst sitting, as this will restrict blood supply. If you get cramp or 'pins and needles' in your legs this is a sign that you have been sitting in an awkward position with poor blood flow.

Insufficient lighting or too much brightness can cause eyestrain. Choose even light levels, preferably with natural daylight from a window.

Regulate the temperature of the room so that you are not cold but not so warm that it makes you sleepy.

Find somewhere you can have peace and quiet. If you are in a noisy environment, experiment with active noise control headphones. These produce an anti-noise signal that cancels out ambient noise. You could even use earplugs or industrial ear-defenders that will physically exclude noise but may be less comfortable to wear.

Try to minimise interruptions. Get a 'do not disturb' sign for your door or even lock yourself in your office or study as long as you can do so without contravening fire safety rules. Unplug or switch off your phone.

Pleasant surroundings are important. Reading should be as pleasurable as possible. If it becomes a drudge you will derive far less benefit from it. How often have you been to the library, especially at a university, and found that half of the people studying there were either bored to tears or struggling to stay awake?

Your emotional state

If you're worrying about something whilst reading this will be a distraction, nagging at the back of your mind. It is a good idea to write down anything on your mind before a reading or study period. The act of literally setting aside thoughts means you can focus much more of your attention on the text. Another approach is called the Sedona Method. Basically this involves removing negative emotional content by bringing it into your conscious mind and then letting go. Think about your problems or distractions and ask yourself three questions: 'Can I let this go?', 'Will I let it go?', 'When?', to which the answers should be: 'Yes', 'Yes' and 'Now'.

If you're fit and well, in a good environment and have the right state of mind you can concentrate on the next step of reading.

3 Comprehension

By comprehension, we mean integration of the information within the book. For example, if you're reading a novel and certain characters, events and locations are introduced early in the story then you need to comprehend these elements in order to make sense of the plot when they are referred to later. In a study book, concepts will often be introduced at the start of a section and then expanded in subsequent chapters. If you do not comprehend the concepts when introduced, you will struggle with the future references to them.

If you have to read in a non-native language, this will often be a barrier to your comprehension. As speed reading involves taking in information at very near to the speed of thought, you must be able to think in the language that you are reading. If you have to mentally translate what you read then this will act as a bottle-neck in the same way that a production line can only work at the speed of the slowest step.

brilliant example

Several years ago, I ran a speed reading course as part of the graduate induction programme for a bank in the Netherlands. The majority of the students were native Dutch speakers but the course was conducted in English. Most the delegates improved their speed but then hit a plateau. This was their speed of translation. It was interesting that two students in the group continued to increase their speed by great leaps. One of them was English and the other had spent several years studying in America so was immersed in the language to the extent that he habitually thought in English.

Wherever possible try to get translations of books in your first language. If the publisher has done the translation for you, it will make your task of reading much easier.

4 Understanding

Understanding differs from comprehension in that it relates your existing knowledge to new information acquired from the text. You are combining your own ideas, experiences and pre-conceptions with those expressed by the author. Understanding can also include comparing viewpoints of different authors from a variety of books on any given subject or bringing together differing subjects to take a holistic or interdisciplinary approach.

If you are studying, examiners are aiming to determine the depth and breadth of your knowledge. The difference between an A grade and an A* is often demonstrating that you can see how a subject fits into a broader context and connects to other areas. This is what understanding is all about. I will explain more about this later (Chapter 9).

It is understanding that leads to innovation, progress and new ideas.

5 Storage

If your purpose for reading is simply to pass the time then storage becomes less important. However, if you are reading for study or for work then it is vital to remember what you have read. Reading without storage largely defeats the point of reading in the first place. It's important to store information in such a way that it is easy to retrieve. Apply effective note-taking strategies that use keywords and highlighting or, even better, a technique such as Mind Mapping. For long-term memory it is important to review your notes regularly and even use memory techniques to embed the information more strongly. We will cover retention in more detail later (Chapters 8 and 9).

In addition to memory or storage in your head, information can be stored on your computer, in a library or on a bookshelf. How much time have you spent looking for a particular book, or a file on your computer that you remember using years ago but have completely lost track of? Computer search tools like Spotlight on my Mac are somewhat useful. The problem is that, as it looks for keywords, it can often find these in a completely different context in irrelevant files. Always try to use logical filenames and save things in the right folder. I must admit to being guilty of saving a lot of files to the desktop and then, when it gets too cluttered, copying everything into a single folder. This leads to files from disparate projects being lumped together in a haphazard manner resulting in wasted time searching.

6 Recall

Have you ever gone into an exam after having studied all the relevant material yet, when faced with the questions, your mind has gone blank? Maybe you have had an interview where you knew all the answers but couldn't give them when required.

This happened to me when I was interviewed for a place at Cambridge University after leaving school. I was faced with a panel of interviewers and asked detailed mathematics questions. Very shortly after I left the room, I suddenly realised why they had asked the specific questions they did and that they built a trigonometric identity. I hadn't spotted this in the interview. I knew I had blown my chance and wouldn't be offered a place. My storage was perfect but, due to the stress of the situation, my recall was far from it.

It is important to be able to recall information when required or at least to know where to access it easily. Recall is only as good as the source of information stored. Beware of relying on a single source, especially on the internet, as accuracy is not guaranteed. I remember when composer Ronnie Hazlehurst, who was responsible for many well-known TV theme tunes, sadly died in October 2007. Several obituaries wrongly claimed he had written the song *Reach* for the band S Club 7. The source of the error was an anonymous entry on Wikipedia. Journalists at *BBC News*, the *Guardian*, the *Independent* and *The Times*, amongst others, were all caught out by the hoax.

7 Communicating, applying and creating

If you read something and do nothing with it, what was the point of reading it in the first place?

We usually need to do something with the information that we acquire from text. This could be giving a presentation, raising issues at a meeting, answering an exam question or writing an essay.

Alternatively, your reading may be used as a foundation for future study or lifelong learning. Many people have the misguided opinion that we stop learning when we leave school. Quite the opposite is true. We should continue to learn throughout life.

'I have never let my schooling interfere with my education.'

Mark Twain

Another false belief is that if you continue to study and learn throughout your life, your brain will get full up. This perception is based on a false analogy of the brain as a filing cabinet where the more paper you put in, the less space there is left. In fact the brain is synergetic in operation. This means that the whole is greater than the sum of the parts. Whenever you have a thought, a network of brain cells signal to each other by releasing neurotransmitter chemicals across the gaps, called synapses, between each cell and the next. This memory trace, as it is called, is fleeting and fragile. However, if the same thought, action or skill is repeated the connections become stronger. More chemicals are available for release next time. This phenomenon, called 'long-term potentiation', leaves the memory trace a little stronger. Over time, new connections grow to make a multi-channel pathway in the brain.

You can think of this process by an analogy of crossing a field of wheat. If you try to walk across a crop field, the first time will be quite difficult as you have to part and tread down stems. If someone follows you along the same pathway it will be easier. Someone following them will find it easier still. Eventually there will be a wide new footpath across the field.

What has this got to do with the amount that you can learn? All learning is based on connections of brain cells. The more connections there are, the easier it is to form new connections. If you have a conceptual framework in place you can associate new knowledge more easily. The more you learn the more you can learn and the easier it becomes.

Even if you are reading simply to keep abreast of current developments in your field or the world in general, you will probably want to discuss what you have learnt with friends or colleagues. Being able to communicate what you have read with appropriate detail and rephrase it in your own words is a very important skill.

'The more you read,
the more things you will know.
The more that you learn,
the more places you'll go.'

Dr Seuss

STOP YOUR TIMER NOW (word count 2,787)

Comprehension questions

1 What are the two main methods for learning to read? [2]

2 Name the seven steps of reading. [7]

3 Name one of the factors that can interfere with assimilation. [1]

Check your answers in Appendix 1.

Number of points × 10 = % comprehension

Calculation
Timer reading
  Minutes:
  Seconds: divide by 60 and add to whole minutes

2,787/time =   Speed (words per minute)

Enter your comprehension and speed in the chart in the Introduction.

↗)brilliant) exercise

You will need a friend or colleague to help you with this exercise. It relies on observation of how the eyes move. It is interesting that you cannot see your eyes moving in a mirror. If the brain did not edit out the information coming from the eyes as they move you would see blurred images, like you get if you shake a camera when taking a picture on a long exposure.

Face your partner and hold the book up so that they can see your eyes whilst you read. Ask them to watch your eyes carefully. Read about half a page of text at your normal speed. Then do the same thing trying to push yourself to read faster. Once your partner has watched you, exchange roles and repeat the exercise. ▶

Discuss what you observed. This will be described in detail in the next chapter.

CHAPTER 3

Understanding your eyes

START YOUR TIMER NOW

The simple observation of how the eyes of a slow or average reader move can have a very dramatic effect on reading speed. Once you have identified the characteristics that lead to slow reading you can eradicate or reverse these behaviours and hence speed up. In this chapter I will discuss four elements that slow down reading and then the four inverse techniques to immediately increase your speed.

If you watch medal-winning athletes in the marathon, 5,000 or 10,000 metres, what do they look like as they cross the finishing line? Some words that come to mind are effortless, elegant, smooth, graceful, comfortable, confident, natural and rhythmic. In contrast, those that come in last are hesitant, negative, laboured, washed-up, stilted, disjointed, lacking confidence and often looking angry or cheated. If you apply the techniques described below as you read you'll start to feel more like the winning athletes than the ones that trail behind. Everything becomes easy and almost effortless, and that is only the beginning.

 'Reading is to the mind as aerobic training is to the body.'

Tony Buzan

Observations of how the eyes move

In the exercise at the end of the last chapter, you probably observed three main actions that your eyes perform when reading.

Pausing on individual words

Did you see your partner's eyes jumping from word to word, briefly pausing on each? It looks a bit like an old-fashioned type-writer juddering across the page until it gets to the end and you push back the carriage to start the next line. In order for the eyes to take a mental 'photograph' they must be still. Imagine looking out of a train window at a sign on the platform as it goes through a station. In order to read it you must either move your head or dart your eyes left and right to compensate for the motion of the train. You are often unaware that your eyes are moving and pausing as this happens subconsciously. As your gaze flits from visual scene to scene, the brain edits out the blurred image that occurs whilst the eyes are travelling and you only perceive what they take in whilst stationary.

Each time the eye comes to rest, it takes in an image of the word that it is focused on. These pauses are called 'fixations' and last between a quarter and one-and-a-half seconds. Slow readers have a long duration for each fixation, focusing on one or two words at a time, occasionally taking two fixations to assimilate longer or unfamiliar words.

Skipping backwards

Did you notice the eyes darting backwards before the end of a line? This has two causes, backskipping and regression. Backskipping is the habitual re-reading of what has just been read. Regression is the conscious process of re-reading, caused by uncertainty of what was read and the desire to clarify.

Wandering

Finally, you may have noticed the eyes wandering off the line or the page entirely. Even if your eyes do not stray, your attention often will. You feel you have been reading but you have actually been thinking about what you will have for lunch, your wife/ husband or girl/boyfriend, or an important essay, meeting or appointment. It is perfectly natural for your mind to stray, especially when reading slowly. Your brain craves stimulation. If the information reaching it from the eyes is coming in at a snail's pace, it is bound to go off into your imagination to seek something else to pay attention to.

Translating the slow reading habits into speed techniques

Each of these three elements of slow reading can be improved or eliminated to increase your speed.

Maintaining focus

Have you ever seen someone look at their watch and then asked them the time? They almost invariably look at their watch again before telling you. When they looked the first time they didn't focus sufficiently well to register the time in their memory. It is amazing how little we actually notice. If you ask someone to look at their watch to tell you the time and then ask if their watch face has Roman numerals, Arabic numbers or even no numbers at all, they will probably be unable to tell you. They may not even notice whether the watch has a second hand or not.

There is a famous demonstration of this on the internet used to promote road safety. Just Google 'dancing bear basketball' and you can watch the video. It consists of a basketball game. You are asked to watch closely and count the number of times the ball is passed by one of the teams. Because your focus is on counting, this is all you notice. If you watch it a second time you will notice that in the middle of the game, someone in a bear costume came onto the court and did a dance. Even though this was really blatant you would have almost certainly missed it. This phenomenon is known as inattention blindness. Professor Richard Wiseman from the University of Hertfordshire has also demonstrated a similar phenomenon known as change blindness. You can find this at **www.quirkology.com/USA/ Video_ColourChangingTrick.shtml**. I won't spoil it by telling you what happens.

Visual and mental focus are very important factors in your success in reading. People often complain of an inability to concentrate. In actual fact they are continually concentrating. Some of the time they are concentrating on the page, at other times they are concentrating on the ceiling, an attractive individual that has just walked past, or their inner thoughts and imagination. It is just a matter of deciding where you will direct your concentration. You can focus your concentration in various ways. Think about why you are reading. Is it to reach a practical goal such as to pass an exam, achieve promotion at work or some other aspiration? If you can't answer why you are reading, there is probably little point in doing so. We will consider motivation in more detail below (Chapter 4).

Have you ever read a novel where you were totally absorbed in the story, so much so that you 'couldn't put the book down'? In that case it is the story that captivates your attention but it is equally possible to be captivated by non-fiction. The faster you read, the more engaged you become in the material. If you read at close to the speed of thought you have little time for your attention to wander. To maintain focus simply tell yourself that you will keep your eyes and attention on the page.

Reducing the duration of fixations

Imagine you are driving down a Swiss autobahn at 80 miles an hour. Suddenly you go round a curve in the road and see an entirely new vista before you. In a split second you are able to notice cars and lorries in front of you, trees and flowers beside the road and mountains in the distance. If you can take in all this visual information virtually instantaneously and effortlessly it is an easy task to fixate on a word for a quarter of a second whilst reading.

Psychological studies using a tachistoscope (a device that displays an image for a specific amount of time), conducted chiefly by the Royal Air Force, showed that with training an average person can identify minute images flashed on the screen for only one five-hundredth of a second (2 ms). Although the images used were of aeroplanes, the results have implications for reading.

The shorter your fixation time, the faster you read. If you currently take one second per fixation, reducing this to half a second will double your speed or reducing to a quarter of a second will give a four-fold increase.

Taking in meaningful chunks of words

The number of fixations can have a massive impact on your speed. As we have seen, slow readers take in one or two words at a time. With practice your eyes can focus on four to six words in a single fixation, depending on length. So if you take in twice as many words in each fixation you can double your speed again.

Chunking is a well-known technique in memory. Short-term memory can hold between five and nine pieces of data at the same time. If you have an eleven-digit phone number this is too much to store. Chunking overcomes this problem by breaking information into manageable blocks. If you have to remember the number 01825708263, it is easier to memorise it as three chunks, 01825 708 263. This 'takes up' three spaces in memory rather than eleven.

Many readers avoid taking in groups of words at high speed because they are afraid that they will miss vital information. When I was at primary school we were given cards with a piece of text to read and comprehension questions. I still remember the exact phrase used was 'Read this passage slowly and carefully'. It was written in good faith at the time but has doubtlessly damaged the prospects of countless would-be fast readers. If you believe that the way to good comprehension is to read 'slowly and carefully' with one word at a time and you get poor results, you will inevitably try harder. You'll read even more slowly, more carefully and your results will get worse. The more you try, the worse it gets and you will be locked into a downward spiral. One of the most destructive forces in learning is believing a false formula to be true and then putting energy into pursuing it. If you believe the best way to escape from quicksand is to struggle you will sink. If you are a strong, fit athlete and able to struggle more vigorously you will sink even faster.

When you take in groups of words, try to take in meaningful chunks. These act like building blocks that the brain assembles to make sense of what you are reading. Doing this will massively boost comprehension and you will end up with a positive upward spiral.

 'I say, which would you rather do: eat a bowl of rice kernel by kernel, or take a spoonful to get a good taste?'

Evelyn Wood, speed reading pioneer

Avoid backskipping

Backskipping and regression account for a 10 to 20 per cent reduction in potential reading speed. Research shows that regression is unnecessary in most cases as meaning can more easily be clarified by the following sentences and paragraphs.

Trust that you will take in information by reading each sentence once.

When I was learning to ski, I had a brief period where I would be hurtling down a slope, seemingly doing well but would shift my weight too far back and effectively sit down, coming to an ignominious stop. It felt like I was going too fast. Once I accepted that I could travel that fast and control my descent, coming to a stop at the bottom, I was able to improve. It was all about trust.

Believe in yourself, believe that you will assimilate and comprehend information without the need to re-read sentences and you will succeed. As Henry Ford said, 'If you think you can do a thing or think you can't do a thing, you're right.'

brilliant dos and don'ts

Do
✔ Take in groups of words.
✔ Take less time per fixation.
✔ Trust yourself that you will comprehend material reading it once.

Don't
✘ Backskip or re-read sentences.
✘ Let your attention or eyes wander off the page.

STOP YOUR TIMER NOW (word count 1,905)

Comprehension questions

1 How long does an average fixation take? [1]
2 Name three factors that lead to slow reading. [3]

3　We are always concentrating but this is not always directed at our reading. True or False? [1]

4　According to studies by the RAF, how long did it take to recognise an image of an aircraft flashed on a screen? [1]

5　With practice how many words can be taken in with a single fixation? [1]

6　What phrase was taught to me at school to aid comprehension that was actually bad advice? [1]

7　If you think you have missed something when reading, which of the following should you do?

　(a)　Take a break

　(b)　Continue reading

　(c)　Go back and reread the sentence or paragraph [1]

8　What percentage reduction in potential speed is caused by backskipping and regression? [1]

Check your answers in Appendix 1.

Number of points × 10 = % comprehension

Calculation

Timer reading

　Minutes:

　Seconds:　　　　　　　divide by 60 and add to whole minutes

1,905/time =　　　　　Speed (words per minute)

Enter your comprehension and speed in the chart in the Introduction.

CHAPTER 4

Managing your motivation and state of mind

START YOUR TIMER NOW

brilliant definition

Motivation
Motivation can be defined as 'an internal desire and force that
drives us to accomplish tasks and goals.'

Motivation is a very common problem when reading,
especially for dry academic texts. Almost every student
has at one time or another dreaded picking up a study
book with the prospect of utter boredom.

When I was at university I remember having 'Summer Reading'
prescribed by some of the lecturers. I once spent many hours of
a holiday in Northumberland reading about the 'forces between
molecules'. I did everything wrong in those days. I didn't plan
my reading and did it in an environment where there were many
things I would much rather be doing. Every time I picked up the
book the drudgery got worse and my reading speed got slower.
How I wish I had known about speed reading techniques back
then!

If you find a subject boring, consider the philosophy of Leonardo
da Vinci who said that everything is in some way connected to

everything else. If you believe this to be true then if you are interested in one thing you are, by definition, interested in everything. The moment you declare a lack of interest in something you sever part of the web of interconnections. Imagine taking a pair of scissors to a spider's web. You only have to cut a few threads to completely destroy the structure. Children are the best learners in the world and are interested in absolutely everything. As we get older we make choices that one by one imprison our curiosity and natural desire to explore. Next time you are in a library, try picking up a book from a section that you would usually walk past. You never know where this will lead.

Reading distractions

We often set out with good intentions but make up fantastically creative 'work avoidance strategies' under the pretence of preparation.

Have you ever sat down to read and then thought that you should really tidy your desk, as it is better to have a good reading environment? You notice that your chair is squeaking so you spend half an hour searching in the garage for some oil. Then you realise that you're hungry and you certainly couldn't concentrate on your reading with a rumbling stomach. You go to the kitchen for a snack that turns into a main meal, after which you feel sleepy so watch a bit of television while you digest your food. You notice your favourite show is about to come on so decide to watch that before getting down to work. Before you know it, it's too late to start so you have an early night so that you will be fresh to begin the next day.

It is only natural that we procrastinate, put off and avoid doing something that we dislike. Reading and learning should be something that you look forward to. If you really can't accept that a textbook could ever be fun to read you can at least make the process painless by spending less time doing it.

The old adage, 'How do you eat an elephant?' – 'One bite at a time' definitely applies.

Why are you reading?

One of the biggest challenges to motivation is not considering why you are reading. You will nearly always have a medium- or long-term goal that your reading will help you to achieve. Are you studying for a qualification that will help you towards a specific career or promotion? Whatever your ultimate goal is, keep it in mind. Visualise what it will feel, look and sound like to achieve it. If you are passionate about achieving something you will do whatever is needed and reading will be a small part of that.

Remember to break your big goal into manageable, achievable steps in the same way that you break reading a big book down into smaller sections. If each stepping stone gets you nearer to your goal they take on extra significance and seem more worthwhile pursuing.

Give yourself rewards for achieving minor reading goals. This can be a simple thing like a special coffee, a few minutes playing 'Angry Birds' or logging on to Facebook or Twitter. Always stay alert to how long your rewards last. It is all too easy to spend an hour enjoying a reward for 45 minutes' focused work.

Managing your state of mind

You can regulate your energy levels by listening to music prior to reading. You may have noticed that Olympic athletes often enter the stadium wearing ear buds from their MP3 players. They have specific tunes that help them to get into the 'zone' for peak performance. Music causes a frequency-following response to induce various brainwave states. Our brains are essentially a combination of electricity and chemistry and brainwaves are voltage fluctuations resulting from ionic current flows within the neurons (brain cells). These are recorded from multiple electrodes placed on the scalp in a technique called electro-encephalography (EEG). Brainwaves are broadly grouped into four categories according to frequency:

1   Beta: 13–25 Hz (cycles per second) – when you are wide awake, talking, delivering a presentation or working on a logical problem.

2   Alpha: 8–12 Hz – a state of relaxed alertness that links best to the subconscious mind. Alpha state is best for storing long-term memories.

3   Theta: 4–7 Hz – the early stages of sleep. Theta is often associated with creativity.

4   Delta: 0.5–3 Hz – deep sleep.

Eight times World Memory Champion, Dominic O'Brien, explains how he uses technology to help balance his own brain and those of his clients.

'I regularly measure the performance of my brain using EEG whether I am relaxed, reading, memorising or recalling information.

Neuro feedback involves being wired up to a computer via EEG and playing games using the power of the brain. For example, if you are a stressed-out trader in the city producing far too much Beta in the higher frequency range and are becoming absent-minded then you would play a game that encourages you to produce slower speeds such as Alpha and Theta waves. This might involve watching a ball move through a maze. The ball will only start to move if you can reduce the Beta and promote Alpha activity. So the incentive is to mentally relax. After several sessions of this type of entrainment your brain learns to shift gear on its own and begins to relax. With Alpha frequencies securely reinstalled your memory starts to work efficiently once more. Conversely, if you were suffering from attention problems then you would benefit from a little higher frequency Beta training. This time the ball would only move through the maze if you reduced your Theta activity and increased low Beta. This carrot and stick feedback allows your brain to tune into frequencies that are conducive to relaxing, focusing, reflecting and making decisions.'

 brilliant example

An example of the power of Theta state of mind is documented by nineteenth-century chemist, August Kekulé. The chemical compound benzene (C_6H_6) was discovered in 1825 by Michael Faraday but its structure was a mystery. It was less reactive than expected and presented a puzzle to chemists. One evening in 1864, Kekulé sat watching the fire, beginning to doze off. The flames danced like snakes before his eyes and, as he watched, one curled round and bit its own tail forming a ring. This creative insight led Kekulé to form the hypothesis that benzene is a hexagonal ring.

Albert Einstein was fond of thought experiments where he would follow his imagination to find new insights. When he was 16, he daydreamed about chasing after a beam of light until he caught up to it. At that point, he reasoned, the light wave would appear frozen. This was impossible according to the thinking at the time and eventually led Einstein to the theory of special relativity.

'I insist on a lot of time being spent, almost every day, to just sit and think. That is very uncommon in American business. I read and think. So I do more reading and thinking, and make less impulse decisions than most people in business. I do it because I like this kind of life.'

Warren Buffett

The best state for learning is in the Alpha to Theta range. To reach this, try listening to baroque music such as Vivaldi's *The Four Seasons* or works by Bach, Corelli, Handel or Telemann. If you are not into classical music, artists such as Enya, Loreena McKennitt or Jacques Loussier offer good alternatives. The brain synchronises to the music and takes you into the desired state of mind. There are also devices on the market that play tones through headphones and flash lights mounted on glasses that are designed to achieve the same thing. Dominic O'Brien again explains:

'Audio Visual Entrainment or AVE involves wearing glasses containing a set of Light Emitting Diodes, LEDs, which flash at varying speeds. Headphones are worn with accompanying sound pulses. The frequency of the light and sound can be set to match any desired brainwave pattern. For example, if you want to train to access the Alpha state you would the set the programme to a 10 hertz frequency and with eyes closed you would sit back in a comfy chair and let your brainwaves tune into a relaxing Alpha pattern of flashing lights for about 20 minutes.

It is now accepted as a non-invasive therapy that can help reduce and in some cases eliminate a wide range of neurological disorders such as ADD, ADHD, migraine, insomnia and depression.

This form of brainwave tuning is well-documented and is known as the Frequency Following Response. AVE is an extremely powerful tool for resetting and conditioning the brain back into good working order and I would recommend that every home has one. One of my clients who has her own light and sound machine describes it as a 'defrag' for her brain. She feels as though the light and sound patterns return her brain to its natural default settings.'

If you need to boost your energy levels, you can listen to upbeat music of your choice. Original research in 1993 by Frances Rauscher, Gordon Shaw and Katherine Ky from the University of California, Irvine, indicated that listening to compositions by Mozart increased performance in spatial reasoning tests. However, later studies seem to indicate that, from a brain training point of view, there is nothing special about Mozart and any music that is pleasant or interesting and puts you in a good mood is likely to have the same effect. In fact, when working with teenagers, Oasis actually out-performed Mozart.

brilliant tip

Although listening to music is a good mental preparation, it is not advisable to do so whilst reading. Music, especially a tune with lyrics, acts as a distraction and you want to give your entire focus to the reading material.

Another way to reach a desired state of mind is a technique known as anchoring. The theory behind this is that a physical or mental state can be linked to a particular stimulus. If a particular song was playing when you broke up with someone and you hear that song on the radio years later, it brings back all the feelings. I have several pieces of music that act as very strong anchors for me, from deep sadness to energising feelings and hilarity. Russian psychologist Ivan Pavlov first showed the link between stimulus and state of mind in 1901 in a classic experiment. The experiment was conducted by ringing a bell whenever Pavlov fed his dogs. Eventually, they were conditioned to salivate whenever a bell was rung, even in the absence of food. The stimulus does not have to be a sound or physical action and even smells can act as anchors. You can create a conditioned response by making a specific action, such as squeezing your earlobe or touching your shoulder, whenever you find yourself in a good frame of mind for effective reading. Eventually the action and brain state will become linked, so to trigger an effective state you simply perform the physical action.

You can alleviate stress and improve your state of mind by simple visualisation. Find somewhere quiet and comfortable to sit, away from distractions. Close your eyes and breathe in through your nose and out through your mouth. With each out breath give a little sigh and count slowly backwards from ten to one. With each number feel the stress drain out of you. Imagine being somewhere tranquil where you can feel relaxed and safe. Perhaps on a warm tropical beach, in a forest or in the mountains. Imagine the sights, smells, sounds, tastes and physical sensations as if you were really there. Spend as long as you like. When you're ready to return, count slowly back from one to ten, the scene fading with each number. When you reach ten, open your eyes and feel refreshed and relaxed.

brilliant example

GCSE student Nissa would prepare for exams by imagining sitting in her bedroom stroking her beloved cat. She felt safe, relaxed and in a far more productive state going in to the examination room than her classmates who were getting each other worked up into a mild state of panic. She did very well at school and college. She now has a PhD.

Motivation by imagination

Another way to motivate yourself is to imagine that something valuable or important is at stake. This will increase your level of arousal, which refers to the overall readiness to engage in an activity. For example, you could imagine that you are taking part in the World Speed Reading Championship and there is a million pound prize to the winner. A hush descends across the expectant crowd of spectators as each competitor, seated at their individual desks, are handed a previously unpublished book. In time-honoured fashion the adjudicator announces, 'Neurons at the ready … Go!' There is a flurry of activity as each competitor flips back the cover and begins to move their pointers across the pages. After 22 minutes the first competitors are putting their books down and the times are recorded by official observers armed with stopwatches. Next come the comprehension questions. Have the competitors overstretched themselves? Can they remember the plot and the small details they are tested on? Their responses are marked to declare a winner.

There really is a World Speed Reading Championship, although not yet with a million pound prize, won six times by former English teacher Anne Jones from England.

Even though the above example is just imagined, with motivation you will still put extra energy and focus into your reading and as a result read much faster.

STOP YOUR TIMER NOW (word count 2,447)

Comprehension questions

1 What did Leonardo da Vinci say that is relevant to interest when reading or studying? [1]

2 List the four brainwave states in order from lowest to highest frequency. [4]

3 What brainwave state is best for learning? [1]

4 Listening to music with lyrics whilst reading aids concentration. True or False? [1]

5 Name two ways to induce a state of relaxation. [2]

6 List one way to improve motivation. [1]

Check your answers in Appendix 1.

Number of points $\times$ 10 = % comprehension

Calculation
Timer reading
   Minutes:
   Seconds: divide by 60 and add to whole minutes

2,447/time =   Speed (words per minute)

Enter your comprehension and speed in the chart in the Introduction.

↗) brilliant exercise

In the next chapter we consider peripheral vision. To determine how wide and high your peripheral vision is we will conduct a little experiment. You can do this on your own but it will be much easier if you can work with a friend or colleague.

Sit facing each other, close enough that your knees almost touch. Look straight ahead, focusing on your friend's forehead. Ask your friend to place their hands slightly in front of your face either side of your eyes and to wiggle their index fingers. They should then draw their arms apart, still wiggling their fingers, until you can no longer see the movement. You will be surprised just how wide your field of vision is. The reason for the wiggling is that your peripheral vision is especially sensitive to movement.

Repeat the exercise, this time moving vertically. Notice whether one hand moves out of your field of vision sooner than the other.

Finally, switch roles so that you each have a chance to measure the other's field of vision.

If you choose to do this on your own, make sure that you are in a private space. Otherwise you will get some very odd looks as you stretch your arms out and wiggle your fingers!

CHAPTER 5

Developing your peripheral vision

START YOUR TIMER NOW

n this chapter I will explore how to make the most of your focused and peripheral vision.

A large percentage of your eyes' light receptors are devoted to your peripheral vision so it makes sense to use this largely untapped resource when reading. Although you can't see colour or fine detail in the periphery of your visual field it is still a very valuable tool to help build both speed and comprehension. I will explain how one very simple change to how you read can greatly improve the effective use of your vision. I will also expose the myth that seeing is just a function of the eyes and explore how the brain plays as great, or even greater, role in seeing and reading as the eyes.

Wider than a page

You should have noticed from the exercise at the end of the previous chapter that your peripheral vision is very wide. When working vertically, did the hand above your head disappear closer than the one below? This is usually the case as your brow gets in the way.

It makes sense that we have a wider field of vision horizontally as our eyes are arranged side by side on our heads rather than one above the other. From an evolutionary point of view, it was important for our hunter-gatherer ancestors to be sensitive to potential predators such as sabre-toothed tigers stalking them from either the left or right. It was far less likely that they would be attacked from above by an eagle swooping down from the sky.

If you look at a rabbit's eyes, you will notice that they are on the sides of its head. This gives it almost 360-degree vision. Rabbits are very vulnerable to predation by foxes, cats, dogs and even weasels and ferrets, so need to react very quickly to run from danger. On the other hand, predators' (such as cats') eyes face forward, offering a wide field of overlapping sight. In the area of binocular vision, depth perception and distance assessment their vision is greater than any other carnivore's, which contributes to their remarkable hunting skill. However, a fearful cat's pupils will be fully dilated to create a wider field of vision and take in as much of the surroundings as possible.

The fact that your field of vision is much wider than a page has important consequences for reading.

The science of seeing

The optics of your eye act a lot like a camera. Light initially passes through the cornea, a clear cover that protects the eye, before entering through the pupil, an opening a little like a camera's aperture. The iris regulates pupil size. This is the coloured part of the eye that expands and constricts to allow more or less light in. It is interesting that the iris not only responds to intensity of light but it also reacts to emotions. If you see something interesting or attractive your iris will constrict to widen your pupil. Chinese jade traders used this fact to gauge customers' interest in particular stones and hence quote an appropriate price.

Once light has passed through the pupil it enters the lens. This changes shape to focus nearby or distant objects upside down on the retina, a series of light-sensitive cells lining the back of the eye. These are predominately of two types: the rods and cones.

Rods function mainly in dim light and provide black-and-white vision, while cones support daytime vision and the perception of colour. Cones are more densely packed in the centre of the macula region of the retina in a small pit called the fovea. This is responsible for sharp central vision, necessary for reading. If an object is large and thus covering a large angle, the eyes must constantly shift their gaze to subsequently bring different portions of the image into the fovea (as in reading with a book close to your eyes).

Although I have used a camera analogy this is far from the reality of how the eye and brain work in combination with each other. Seeing takes place primarily in the brain. The visual cortex at the back of the brain is divided into regions that specialise in processing different aspects of the image. What the eyes actually deliver is a very sharp, coloured central image with less sharp but very wide peripheral vision. This includes two 'holes' that correspond to the blind spot where the optic nerve joins the retina in each eye and where there are no photoreceptors. The brain fills in the blanks and gives us a perception of the world. Most so-called 'optical' illusions actually occur in the brain rather than the optics of the eyes. Segall et al. (1966) found that people from Zulu tribes were unable to perceive the Müller-Lyer illusion, devised by the German sociologist in 1889 (see Figure 5.1 below). This is probably because their visual environment contains few rectangles, straight lines and regular corners and so their brains are not sensitised to these.

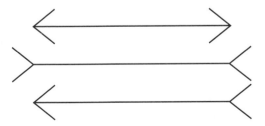

Figure 5.1 The Müller-Lyer illusion – all three lines are the same length

When you consider what an amazing job the brain does with limited information, you shouldn't worry about missing the odd word when reading!

So what does this practically mean for reading?

One consequence of the eye's optics is that, if you hold a book, or digital device, too close to your eyes, you are not making the most of your visual system.

Imagine holding a book a couple of centimetres from your eyes, almost touching your nose. You will just about be able to focus on it and see perhaps one or two words.

Now imagine the book at **a** typical distance of about 20 centimetres. You have no trouble focusing on the page but because the book is further away the text appears smaller. A larger area of the page is projected onto the central area of your retina by the eye's optics. You will hence be able to read groups of words.

Finally, if you hold the book at a distance of 50 centimetres you can focus on a much larger area of the page and still see it clearly. Taking in groups of words is far easier and you will be able to take in larger 'visual gulps'. Because of the increased distance of the book, the eyes have to move far less to track across the width of the page. The geometry makes a great improvement to all areas of focused reading.

brilliant tip

When reading, always hold your book or digital device at almost arm's length. As far away as possible, whilst still being comfortable, to focus on and see the text.

If you find it uncomfortable to hold your arm out when reading, especially if you have a heavy book, you can use a bookstand (often sold for recipe books) or even a music stand. If you are reading using an iPad the cover can be folded so that it will stand upright without the need to physically hold it.

What use is peripheral vision?

It is remarkable to think of the ramifications of something as simple as holding the book at a greater distance, but it doesn't stop there. Holding the book at arm's length has the secondary benefit that your peripheral vision is able to work more effectively.

Although not in sharp focus, your peripheral vision still gives your brain useful information. You need your central focus to read each group of words, but peripheral vision can identify paragraph structure, layouts, large headings, the position of illustrations and even some words, as we will see in the exercise at the end of this chapter.

Of the 130 million photoreceptors in each eye, over 80 per cent are devoted to peripheral vision. Have you ever been reading one column of a newspaper or book and noticed that there is a particular word elsewhere on the page or even on the opposite page? You have a sense that it is there but then have to hunt to find it. It will be something important to you that your peripheral vision has spotted and to which your subconscious has been alerted.

Comprehension is improved if you have a general idea of the structure of a page. The main headings and paragraph structure helps create a framework into which the detail is placed. As your peripheral vision can easily take in a whole page, it acts as a scout, previewing what is coming up and helping to provide this framework before you read with your central focus. It gives your brain a starting point upon which to build meaning.

Peripheral vision not only lets you 'see ahead' but also you literally 're-view' what you have just read. Reviewing is one of the prime keys to memory so making use of peripheral vision also helps you remember what you read.

Another added benefit is that you do not have to focus so hard. This can reduce some of the most common ailments associated with reading such as fatigue, eyestrain and headaches. Holding the book at a distance will help you avoid hunching forward or bending your head down to read. Bad posture and neck stress are almost guaranteed to cause neck and back pain and reduce your focus, concentration and the amount of time you can read.

As well as taking in groups of words on a single line you will eventually find that your focused vision is able to take in more than one line at a time. This may sound counterintuitive but when you consider just how much processing the brain does merely to see an image, it is not unreasonable to expect it to make sense of bigger chunks of information. Each group of words works like a jigsaw piece that the brain slots together to make sense of the text. Using a pointer to guide the eyes facilitates this process. We will cover guiding in detail in Chapter 7.

Try to make sure that your reading material is as clear as possible. Avoid old, cheaply printed books where the paper has oxidised and gone yellow. With eBook readers, go for the largest and clearest display you can. Apple's 'Retina display' on the new iPad has 3.1 million pixels, so close together that your eyes can't discern individual ones at a normal viewing distance. Try to read in natural daylight or, if this is not possible, position a light shining over the shoulder opposite the hand you write with to avoid glare and shadows. Try not to have a big difference between overall illumination in the room and lighting of your desk or reading area.

> ### ☀ brilliant tip
>
> If you wear glasses normally or just to read, you should ask your optician about 'occupational lenses'. New technology called 'freeform surfacing' is now available that uses a computer-controlled diamond cutter to create ultra-high-precision lenses. These can be designed to provide easy, close-up focus on small text in the 40–70 cm viewing range without losing sharp focus on immediate and distant surroundings.

STOP YOUR TIMER NOW (word count 1,826)

Comprehension questions

1 Is your field of vision greater horizontally or vertically, and why would this make sense in terms of evolution? [2]

2 Which light-sensitive cells in your retina are responsible for colour vision and where are they most densely packed? [2]

3 How far away from your eyes should you hold a book? [1]

4 What percentage of the photoreceptors in your eyes is responsible for peripheral vision? [1]

5 Name three benefits of using peripheral vision. [3]

6 With practice, focused vision can take in more than one line at a time. True or False? [1]

Check your answers in Appendix 1.

> Number of points × 10 = % comprehension
>
> **Calculation**
> Timer reading
>   Minutes:
>   Seconds: divide by 60 and add to whole minutes
>
> 1,826/time =   Speed (words per minute)   ▶

Enter your comprehension and speed in the chart in the Introduction.

 **exercise**

Once you have read this page turn to page 58 and focus on the word 'a' in the centre of the page that is printed in bold. Hold the book at arm's length and keep your eye focused on that word while you consider the following questions.

Can you:

● See and recognise any words to the left and right of the word you are focusing on? How many on each side?

● Clearly see any words above or below the word you are focusing on?

● Count the number of paragraphs on the page you are focusing on, and on the opposite page?

Are there:

● Page numbers on the page and facing page? Are they at the top or bottom of the pages and in the middle or corners of the pages?

● Any bold or larger headings on the page you are focusing on? How many and can you get the gist of what they say without moving your focus?

● Any on the opposite page? How many?

● Any boxes or shaded areas in the text?

● Any illustrations on the page?

You can see that peripheral vision can take in a lot of information about the page. This is just with a static focus on one word. As you read your focus moves across most of the page so your surrounding peripheral vision is also sweeping across and down the page, taking in more and more information with each fixation.

CHAPTER 6

Skimming, scanning and selective reading

START YOUR TIMER NOW

Scanning and skimming are probably two of the most useful skills in reading as long as you can overcome the fear that you will miss things if you don't read everything with perfect comprehension at all times. Another vital skill that saves a huge amount of time is selective reading. If you understand how specific types of documents are structured you can get to the 'meat' without have to wade through masses of irrelevant detail.

Most of the techniques in this book concern improving speed whilst maintaining or improving comprehension and reading every word. The techniques in this chapter are the exception to this, since they involve trading comprehension for extreme speed. There are many instances when you don't need perfect comprehension and recall of the material that you read. Maybe you are studying and need to 'read around' your subject to give you background information. Perhaps you need to read journals and magazines to keep you abreast of industry trends in your job. You may need to read preparatory documents before going into a meeting at very short notice. Despite the fact that these techniques do not involve reading every word, many people are amazed by how much information they are able to glean from a book or other reading source in a fraction of the time that even 'normal' speed reading takes.

These techniques can also be used to gain an overview of a book before deciding whether to read it from cover to cover. If using traditional reading, starting at page one and progressing through the whole text, you can spend weeks reading only to discover that the book didn't tell you anything useful or relevant. Skimming and scanning form the cornerstone of effective studying that we will explore in depth below (Chapter 9). Finally, you can use these techniques to seek out relevant information on a webpage or large document without having to read the whole thing.

 'Newspapers, magazines, TV and computer screens are some of your windows on the world and, increasingly, the universe. It is possible, by understanding their nature, and some new approaches to them, to increase your efficiency in this area by a factor of ten.'

Tony Buzan, *The Power of Verbal Intelligence*

Scanning

Have you ever used a metal detector? You sweep it over the ground listening for it to beep as soon as it senses buried metal. Scanning reading works in an analogous way. You need to know what you are looking for before you begin and it helps to understand the layout of the book. Take a look at the contents page and index and have a quick flick through the pages as if you were in a bookshop deciding whether to buy it.

The first step is to identify specific questions that you need answered, key words or names that you are looking for.

We all have mental filters on our perception. What we notice or pay attention to is based on many factors, including upbringing, life experiences, beliefs and your current situation. If you are on a diet and hungry, food appears to tempt you in many places.

If you believe that the other queue in the supermarket always moves faster than the one you choose, you will notice every time this happens, reinforcing that belief and ignoring the times when you fly straight through.

If you buy a particular outfit you will suddenly notice that everyone is wearing similar colours or styles. Nothing has changed except that that colour or style has taken on increased importance to you.

In marketing, consumers are also more likely to retain information if a person has a strong interest in the stimuli. If someone is in need of a new car they are more likely to pay attention to an advertisement for a car, while someone who does not need a car may need to see the advertisement many times before they recognise the brand of vehicle.

This filtering is regulated by a part of the brain called the reticular activating system (RAS). The RAS consists of a loose network of neurons and neural fibres running through the brain stem. These neurons connect up with various other parts of the brain. The functions of the reticular activating system are many and varied but perhaps its most important function is its control of consciousness; the RAS is believed to control sleep, wakefulness, and the ability to consciously focus attention on something. In addition, the RAS acts as a filter, dampening down the effect of repeated stimuli. For example, the continuous background hum from a fan or air conditioning unit will quickly be ignored so that you don't notice it. The brain's RAS is constantly monitoring your environment to bring 'important' things to your attention. By identifying what is relevant, you can utilise this natural process to your advantage.

Once you have determined what you're looking for, you can move your eyes across the pages very rapidly. It may help to use your finger to guide your eyes. We will cover guiding in detail in the next chapter. You are not aiming to make total sense of what you are seeing. If you cast your mind back to Chapter 2, this is recognition and assimilation without in-depth comprehension. As you have primed your subconscious to look for something specific this will 'leap out' at you when you come across it. You can mark the page to come back to later or read the appropriate paragraph in detail. Don't allow yourself to fall into the trap of reading large sections or getting engrossed in the text unless it is really relevant. The aim is to survey the whole text in as short a time as possible.

I will build on this technique in a study context later in the text (Chapter 9).

Skimming

Skimming differs from scanning in the important respect that it is less pre-directed. If you watch someone skilled in skipping a stone across a lake you will see it briefly hit the water before bouncing off the surface and continuing to skip. Skimming reading is an analogous process. Your eyes fly over the text, never resting for long and dipping in here and there to take in the odd phrase or sentence. If you prefer, an alternative analogy is a swallow that spends the whole time on the wing. It catches insects in flight and skims over ponds and streams to take a drink, very rarely resting or perching.

Once again, you are not aiming for a high level of comprehension but you should get the gist of a book or report very rapidly. This is especially important either for relatively unimportant documents or if you are particularly time pressured. For example, if you are due in a meeting in ten minutes and you are expected to have read background notes, it would make sense to skim them rapidly rather than go in totally unprepared.

If I receive an email with a long attachment that I am supposed to review, I will often skim read it initially so that I can respond with my initial impression. If I am required to go into more detail at a later date I can speed read in more detail. However, I often find that skimming gave me enough information to serve the purpose without using up too much of my time.

Skimming is ideal for newspapers. Glance at headlines, photos, captions and the first paragraphs of articles. Look at diagrams and summaries if present. Skimming will quickly tell you which articles you want to read and keep. These can be marked with a coloured pen or torn out to read in 'dead time' whilst waiting or travelling. This lets you escape from the nagging annoyance of an unread paper. You can deal with it in 15 minutes and then can always go back and read at a more leisurely pace, for example at the weekend.

Skimming a book before reading it in detail is a really good investment of your time in that it will give you the skeleton of the text that can be fleshed out when you read it in detail. You can see much more clearly how the book fits together and put things in context.

Do you remember in the early days of the internet, before broadband, when everyone had to rely on a dial-up connection? Images were often encoded as 'progressive JPEG files'. This started off by loading a very blocky image that became more detailed as extra data was downloaded. You eventually ended up with a clear photograph but could jump to another page before the picture had finished building up if it turned out to be irrelevant.

brilliant example

Getting an overview of a book can also save a huge amount of time.

A student at Oxford University had spent nearly a year reading a huge textbook before attending a public speed reading course. He had dutifully ▶

started reading on the first page and continued one page at a time, making notes as he went. He was nearly at his wits' end, having got about three-quarters of the way through the book. He felt his head was 'full' and that there had to be a better way to study.

On attending the course he skimmed the book and discovered that the final chapter was a summary of the key points of the whole text. If he had read that first he could have saved himself the majority of the hours devoted to the book. Despite his initial disappointment he was easily able to pass his course armed with his new found skills.

Selective reading

 **brilliant** tip

Being selective with your reading can multiply the time saved from reading faster by a factor of four.

Being selective in what you read is a vital tool to reduce the time spent reading. If you understand how a document is put together you can zone in on the important information, get what you want and move on. Most documents have reams of text that go into far more detail than you need. Think of yourself as a detective like Sergeant Joe Friday, from the radio and television crime drama *Dragnet*, who would always say, 'Just the facts, Ma'am' when he was trying to get information to solve a crime.

Each type of publication or document follows a particular structure. If you know how they are put together you can use this to your advantage.

Court judgments

Court reporters know that judgments follow a standard format. The judge will normally review the case and the main factors in the majority of the document and then deliver their findings in the last paragraph. The reporters start reading from the last page, or even the last paragraph, because they are reading the judgment to report the verdict.

Magazines

Magazines will usually start with an editorial that will either be a personal view on a topical issue or set out what is in that issue depending on the 'house style'. You will then come to the contents page. This will include a list of features, often with a one- or two-line description, highlight the main cover story and regulars such as a news section, letters, events listings, puzzles page, columns, etc. You can glean a lot from the contents page plus a quick skim through the magazine as a whole looking at large headings and glossy photographs, pausing occasionally to mark anything that catches your eye. Tear out pages of interest for later reading and discard the rest.

Scientific papers

Scientific papers always follow a layout so that a reader knows what to expect from each part of the paper, and they can quickly locate a specific type of information. The typical structure is as follows:

> TITLE. The title will help you to decide if an article is interesting, relevant or worth reading. Included in a title are details of what was studied, the kinds of experiments performed, and perhaps a brief indication of the results obtained.
>
> ABSTRACT. Abstracts provide you with a complete, but very succinct, summary of the paper. An abstract contains

brief statements of the purpose, methods, results and conclusions of a study.

INTRODUCTION. An introduction usually describes the theoretical background, covers why the work is important, states a specific research question, and poses a hypothesis to be tested.

METHOD. The method section will help you determine exactly how the authors performed the experiment.

RESULTS. The results section contains the data collected during experimentation.

DISCUSSION AND CONCLUSIONS. The discussion section will explain how the authors interpret their data, how they connect it to other work and will suggest areas of improvement for future research.

ACKNOWLEDGEMENTS. The acknowledgements tell you who, in addition to the authors, contributed to the work.

LITERATURE CITED. This section offers information on the range of other studies cited.

When reading scientific papers, you generally only need to read the title and abstract. If it looks interesting and you need more detail, you may read the discussion. It is only in very rare cases that you will read the whole paper.

Business reports

Well-written business reports follow a similar structure. Typically this includes:

TITLE. This gives a summary about the purpose of the report, the author and date.

CONTENTS. A list of the sections and appendices.

INTRODUCTION AND TERMS OF REFERENCE. The aims and scope of the report.

EXECUTIVE SUMMARY. A one- or two-page summary containing evidence, recommendations and outcomes.

BACKGROUND. The historical situation and reasons for instigating the report or project.

IMPLICATIONS. Issues, implications, facts, figures, evidence (with sources) and possibly results of a tool like SWOT analysis (Strengths, Weaknesses, Opportunities and Threats).

SOLUTION. Options with implications, effects, results, financials, inputs and outputs.

RECOMMENDATIONS. Actions with details of input and outcomes, values, costs and return on investment analysis, if appropriate.

APPENDICES. Additional tables or supporting information.

BIBLIOGRAPHY. References to documents used.

ACKNOWLEDGEMENTS. Credits to people who contributed to the report or whose work was referenced.

In much the same way as reading a scientific paper, a well-structured business report can be tackled by being very selective. Just read the title to see if it is relevant to continue, skim the contents and, if you think it is important, read the executive summary. This will usually be enough. In some cases it may be necessary to read the recommendations to see how this impacts on your work or department. In very rare cases, especially if you disagree with the recommendations, you may wish to read the implications to see what evidence led to the solution but this will almost never be the case.

I learnt this lesson when I worked as a computer programmer in a major bank. Each month a big folder would land on my desk as it was circulated around the department. This included that latest trends and economic forecasts from bank economists, general reports from senior management, sometimes HR policy changes and the internal company magazine. When I started as an eager, inexperienced graduate I would read everything. This lasted a couple of months before I realised that the majority of this was irrelevant. I learnt to discriminate, skim some of it and ignore the majority, then initial the distribution list and pass it on to the next person.

This is the worst possible advice for reading …

"'Where should I begin, please, your Majesty?" he asked. "Begin at the beginning," the King said, gravely, "and go on till you come to the end: then stop.'"

Lewis Carroll, *Alice in Wonderland*

STOP YOUR TIMER NOW (word count 2,599)

Comprehension questions

1   Skimming and scanning are a trade-off between detailed comprehension and extreme speed. True or False? [1]

2   Name one function of the reticular activating system? [1]

3   Describe the difference between scanning and skimming. [1]

4   What technique would you use to go through a newspaper quickly? [1]

5   How much more time can you save by selective reading? [1]

6   Which two sections of a scientific paper are usually all that needs to be read to get what you need from it? [2]

7   Which three areas of a business report are usually all that needs to be read to get what you need from it? [3]

Check your answers in Appendix 1.

Number of points × 10 = % comprehension

Calculation

Timer reading

Minutes:

Seconds: divide by 60 and add to whole minutes

2,599/time =   Speed (words per minute)

Enter your comprehension and speed in the chart in the Introduction.

↗ **brilliant** exercise

In preparation for the next chapter we have another little experiment for which you need to find a friend or colleague. It involves determining the difference between guided and unguided eye movement.

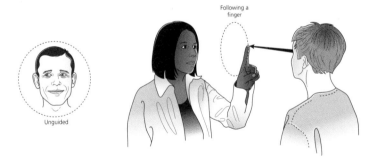

Following a finger

Unguided

Sit or stand facing each other. As your partner watches your eyes, imagine a large, round dinner plate about 40–50 cm in front of your face, as if you were holding it up vertically. Now attempt to slowly move your eyes around the rim of the plate in a clockwise direction. Next, ask your partner to slowly move their finger, describing a similar-sized circle. Follow the tip of their finger with your eyes, as your partner once again observes how your eyes move. Do not move your head, only your eyes.   ▶

Exchange roles so that you both have an opportunity to watch each other's eyes when unguided and when following a finger. Now see the next chapter.

CHAPTER 7

Use of a guide

START YOUR TIMER NOW

 'No matter how busy you may think you are, you must find time for reading, or surrender yourself to self-chosen ignorance.'

Confucius

n this chapter I will explain how to use a reading guide. A slightly apocryphal story states that speed reading pioneer Evelyn Wood stumbled upon this method, when frustrated by her own inability to read faster. While brushing off the pages of the book she had thrown down in despair, she discovered that the sweeping motion of her hand across the page caught the attention of her eyes, and helped them move more smoothly across the page.

A guide can be anything from your finger to a chopstick that gives your eye a point to follow. Use of a guide, once mastered, is one of the most important techniques in speed reading. Anne Jones, World Speed Reading Champion, says, 'The guide makes it easier for our eyes to track across the page. It makes a huge difference to dyslexics and it is what helps me read extremely fast.'

Consider the exercise at the end of the previous chapter: did you notice that in the unguided situation your circle was very angular and misshapen? Did your eyes move more smoothly when they had something to follow?

Imagine a cricket match in which the batsman hits the ball high into the sky. The fielder relies on his ability to track the moving ball with his eyes, predicting its trajectory and getting into position to catch it. If he just saw a series of static images at various points during the ball's flight it would be almost impossible to catch it. This is only natural. Considering evolution and our prehistoric ancestors roaming the plains, being able to follow a moving object was a vital survival skill. If the tribe was to eat, the hunters had to be able to throw a spear at a moving animal such as a wildebeest and hit it sufficiently accurately to kill it. This is a complex feat that can only be achieved if you concentrate and keep your eye on the target as it moves. As we haven't really evolved much since prehistoric times, it makes sense that our eyes and brains are better adapted to hunting than viewing static text.

Do you already use a guide?

In my courses I always ask if anyone uses their finger or a guide to point at words whilst reading. The vast majority of people regardless of age, gender or nationality say 'no'. However, when we investigate further it is often the case that they do in certain circumstances. Think about your reading in the following situations:

Do you ever use your finger when:

- Adding up a column of figures in your head?
- Scanning classified ads in a newspaper?
- Finding a phone number in a printed directory?
- Looking up a word in a dictionary?
- Reading stock prices in the financial pages of a newspaper?

Several of these activities have been largely replaced by internet search engines or apps. Can you think back to whether you did any of these in the past? If you answered 'yes' to any of the above questions then you are instinctively using a guide to help your eyes. It makes sense that you could use a similar technique to help you with your general reading.

Guiding is natural

Can you remember when you were at school and learning to read? Were you taught to point at the words as you read? This is very often the case until one day the teacher says, 'Now you can read well you can take your finger away as it slows you down.'

If your eyes can follow your finger easily and you want to move your eyes faster, then of course it is far better to move your finger faster than to remove the thing that supported your early reading. It is a great shame that teachers, believing that they are acting in the best interests of the children in their care, sometimes make incorrect judgements based on old research and conventional wisdom.

Using a guide automatically assists other techniques

Cast your mind back to the four speed techniques covered in Chapter 3, namely:

1 Focus on the page.
2 Reduce the duration of fixations.
3 Take in groups of words in meaningful chunks.
4 Only move forwards and avoid backskipping.

Following a guide such as your finger assists all these elements of speed reading. If you focus on the tip of your finger and keep this on the page, then your visual focus will also remain on the page.

The faster you move your finger, the faster your eyes will move and hence the shorter your fixation times will be. Make sure that you move your finger in a fluid motion under lines. There is no need to pause and you should avoid tapping as this will be counterproductive, actually lengthening the duration of fixations. It is important to get into a steady rhythm as you move your pointer.

brilliant tip

Try using a metronome to pace yourself. Start a little faster than you are comfortable with, making one sweep of the pointer per tick. When this speed starts to feel more natural, speed up another increment. If you find it too hard to keep up, reduce the speed until it is comfortable and then repeat the exercise of pushing yourself.

If you find your eyes moving ahead of your finger then you are moving it too slowly and can immediately speed up. With practice, over time, you will be able to read substantially faster in comfort.

Start with your pointer a little way in from the left-hand side of the page and stop a little way in from the right and you will automatically take in groups of words at the beginning and end of each line. In fact, experienced speed readers just move their pointers mainly down the middle of the page.

Of course, as long as you only move your finger forwards your eyes will only move forwards.

Initially it may feel very odd to use a pointer but, as you have probably been reading without one for the majority of your life, this is to be expected. Stick with it! You have to unlearn the old habit of letting your eyes drift and train yourself in the new habit of coordinated and deliberate eye movement. It is also possible that your comprehension may drop. The reason for this is that your concentration is split between how to read and the content of what you are reading. Once the process of reading with a guide becomes second nature so that you don't have to think about it, your comprehension will return to the same or higher level that it was originally. This is a bit like learning to drive. When you start it seems impossibly hard to remember 'mirror, signal, manoeuvre', use of the clutch, gears, accelerator, break, indicators, windscreen wipers, headlights and being aware of other road users, all at the same time. Once you have gained experience you can drive whilst listening to the radio, operating sat-nav and conducting a conversation with a passenger or on a 'hands-free' mobile phone, all the time being entirely safe behind the wheel.

Once you become fairly comfortable with a guide, think back to Chapter 5 on peripheral vision. By holding the book further away you can begin to take in chunks of words above and below your central focus as well as to the left and right. It may seem nonsensical to see a line below before you have got to the end of a line you are reading. However, the brain is exceptionally good at piecing information together. You see the words you are concentrating on, you see what you have already focused on and you see what is immediately coming up. This data is combined to give meaning. Experiment moving your guide under two lines at a time. It takes a bit of practice but you may be surprised at just how much you can assimilate.

Equipment

Using your finger as a guide has one major disadvantage. This is that the rest of your hand partially covers the page. As we saw in Chapter 5, your peripheral vision can take in the whole page so covering it will hinder this process. Also, it may start to become a little uncomfortable to point at the text if you are holding the book at the correct distance of about 50 cm from your eyes.

You can guide your eyes more effectively if you use a long, slender pointer, for example, a knitting needle, chopstick, pen, pencil or even a conductor's baton. Remember if you intend to read whilst on aeroplanes that sharp objects will probably be confiscated at security. Experiment with different colours. Some people find it easier to have a coloured tip to follow.

Pointers do not have to be restricted to printed materials. You can use a guide to read Kindles, iPads and other eBook readers. In this case take care to hold your pointer a few millimetres in front of the screen to avoid scratching it or accidentally 'turning' pages. If you are reading from a computer screen you can either use a physical guide or move the mouse pointer under the text. This can be controlled by a mouse, track pad or graphics tablet with stylus depending on what you feel most comfortable with.

Old-fashioned cathode ray tube computer monitors do not lend themselves to using a physical pointer as they flicker but as nearly all systems now use flat liquid crystal displays this is becoming less of an issue.

As we will be using a guide extensively for the next exercise and the rest of the book it is strongly suggested that at the end of this chapter you find a suitable pointer to try.

---

brilliant questions and answers

Q What will people think? Doesn't it look childish?

A Be independent of the concerns of others. There are a lot of prejudices and social conventions surrounding reading and a major stigma associated with illiteracy, yet very few people practise effective reading strategies.

Newcomers to speed reading are sometimes afraid to be seen pointing at words with their fingers when reading in public places. If they are also holding their book at arm's length they feel self-conscious and fear that people will think them backward or in some way mentally inferior. Just because you have a better reading strategy than the people around you doesn't mean this should force you to abandon the most useful components of the technique. Anyway, you will have the last laugh when those peering over the tops of their newspapers see you turning the pages of your book at twice their speed.

If you carry around one chopstick in your handbag or top pocket you may also get some odd looks. I like to joke that I only have one chopstick as I am on a diet! It is easier than trying to explain speed reading to those who like to mock.

As an avid Mind Mapper (see Chapter 9), I also get some stick about always having at least ten coloured pens with me. I just smile to myself in the knowledge that I can take notes and commit them to memory much better than the average person.

American First Lady Eleanor Roosevelt expressed this very well when she said, 'No one can make you feel inferior without your consent.'

Q **How can I stop my eyes moving ahead of the guide or lagging behind?**

A If your eyes are moving ahead of the guide then you are moving it too slowly. Simply speed up. You should aim to get into a steady rhythm taking roughly the same time to sweep across each line (or group of lines). As you get more comfortable with taking in groups of words in chunks you will not need to move your guide as far horizontally but will rather move more down the centre of the page with small lateral movements.

If your eyes are lagging behind the guide there are two possible reasons. First, that you are lacking in the confidence that you can keep up and are still worried about missing important things, in which case try to trust yourself and push your speed. The second possibility is that you are moving the guide too fast. In this case slow down a little and then gradually get faster. It can take a little while to get used to moving your eyes faster. Repeat the 'relativistic' exercise at the end of this chapter to experience faster speeds.

▶

Ⓠ **Does use of a guide work for everyone? I find it uncomfortable.**

Ⓐ It is a biological fact that the eyes naturally work better with something to follow. You have probably been reading without a guide for the majority of your life. That is a very strong habit to break. Stick with the guide. If it feels really uncomfortable, experiment with different types. Maybe a coloured pen would work better than a chopstick. Different people have their own preferences.

STOP YOUR TIMER NOW (word count 2,188)

Comprehension questions

1   Name two cases where many people use a finger to guide their eyes. [2]

2   What are the four techniques covered earlier that a guide can assist with? [4]

3   Why is a slender pointer better than using your finger as a guide? [1]

4   Name three suitable objects to use as a guide. [3]

Check your answers in Appendix 1.

Number of points × 10 = % comprehension

Calculation
Timer reading
  Minutes:
  Seconds: divide by 60 and add to whole minutes

2,188/time =   Speed (words per minute)

Enter your comprehension and speed in the chart in the Introduction.

🔍 brilliant exercise

The brain has an amazing ability to adapt to a situation effortlessly and without you being aware of it. This ability is called 'the relativistic nature of the brain'. Let me explain with an analogy. Imagine you have been driving down the motorway at 70 miles per hour for several hours when suddenly you see flashing lights ahead, a sign saying that there is an accident and you have to slow down to 30mph. Without looking at the speedometer you slow down to what feels like 30 but when you look at it you are actually doing closer to 50. You have become habituated to the faster speed so that 30 feels incredibly slow. The same process can be used to help you increase your reading speed. If you move your pointer at very high speed without attempting to comprehend what your eyes are seeing, when you slow down to what feels like a fast but comfortable speed you will actually be reading faster.

Are you ready to try this?

Turn back to the beginning of this chapter and move your pointer as fast as you possibly can with your eyes following it. If a page contains 500 words, then 4 seconds a page is 7,500 words per minute. This is about 1 ¾ times the world record speed! It is useful to have a means of pacing yourself. Playing a very fast piece of music such as *The Flight of the Bumblebee* by Nikolai Rimsky-Korsakov, *The Race* by Swiss electronic band Yello or *Devil's Gallop* by Charles Williams, famous as the theme tune to the radio serial *Dick Barton – Special Agent* are all good. Move your pointer two sweeps of a line per beat. If you get to the end of the chapter before the music stops, go back to the beginning.

Then immediately, so that you don't have time to lose the energy, go on to Chapter 8 but this time reading with comprehension at what feels a fast but manageable speed. As with the other chapters, calculate your speed. You may be pleasantly surprised.

This exercise is a good mental warm-up before any extended piece of reading. I would recommend doing it fairly regularly as it is a quick and easy way to boost speed.

CHAPTER 8

Comprehension and retention

START YOUR TIMER NOW

 'I took a speed-reading course and read *War and Peace* in 20 minutes. It involves Russia.'

Woody Allen

n this chapter I aim to dispel two commonly held myths about speed reading. First, that as speed increases comprehension goes down (as in the quote above). Secondly, that subvocalisation slows you down and should be eradicated entirely.

As you will see, increased comprehension and speed go hand in hand. Your brain is amazing at discerning meaning even with relatively little information, certainly less than every single word. In fact, slow reading leads to less focus, reduced comprehension and more confusion.

I will show how, when correctly managed, subvocalisation can assist comprehension, retention and enjoyment without impacting on speed. I will also explain how to build knowledge and retain more of what you read.

Comprehension

We saw in Chapter 5 how the brain is capable of making sense of the information received from the eyes by 'filling in the gaps' with its internal mental model of the world. The same thing happens with language. You can get incomplete or distorted information and still make sense of it. For example, can you read the following passage?

> Aoccdrnig to rscheearch at Cmabrigde Uinervtisy, it deosn't mttaer in waht oredr the ltteers in a wrod are, the olny iprmoetnt tihng is taht the frist and lsat ltteer be at the rghit pclae. The rset can be a toatl mses and you can sitll raed it wouthit porbelm. Tihs is bcuseae the huamn mnid deos not raed ervey lteter by istlef, but the wrod as a wlohe.

It is almost as easy to read as correctly written text. This is because the brain is very good at deciphering meaning. It reads words in context rather than isolation. This is another reason why meaningful chunks of information are easier to assimilate. The brain also interprets word shapes rather than reading letter by letter. Read the following sentence as you would normally and make a mental note of how many times the letter 'F' occurs.

FINISHED FILES ARE THE RESULT OF YEARS
OF SCIENTIFIC STUDY COMBINED WITH THE
EXPERIENCE OF YEARS.

There are six. 'Finished', 'Files', 'scientiFic' and 'oF' three times. Did you miss out 'of' when counting? There are two reasons for this. First, 'of' has a 'v' sound so it is not immediately apparent that it contains a letter 'f' when subvocalising. Secondly, 'of' is what is known as a function word. It does not convey information in itself so the brain glosses over it.

Try the following example:

I LOVE PARIS IN THE
THE SPRINGTIME.

Did you notice the repetition of the word 'the'? Because 'I love Paris in the springtime' makes sense the brain automatically decides that is what was written. If you ever do some writing and then proofread it yourself it is very difficult to spot mistakes. You know what you intended to write so you read the meaning rather than the actual words.

If you are able to make sense of the examples on this page, it should be very easy to comprehend correctly written text, even if you miss out or don't understand some of the words. Many people have a phobia of missing important information as they speed read that holds them back. If you think about comprehension like completing a jigsaw, the more pieces of the puzzle you have in place, the easier it is to fill in the gaps. The same is true of reading. When you fear that you haven't understood a sentence, it is always better to keep going. This way you will get more context and a better chance of comprehending. If you get to the end of a chapter and really have no clue what the author was saying then it is worth looking up unfamiliar words but this will very rarely be the case.

People often wrongly assume that speed reading is a trade-off between speed and comprehension. It is logical to assume that as you get faster you take in less. This couldn't be further from the truth.

 'Speed is not most important, but only through speed do you get good comprehension.'

Evelyn Wood, pioneer of speed reading

Why should this be the case?

If

you

slowly

read

one

word

at

a

time

pretty soon you get bored and your mind wonders off in search of something more interesting. Even if you manage to keep your attention on the text, your brain has plenty of time for each word to trigger multiple associations. However, if you read at closer to the speed of thought you have far less time to make up your own meaning and get nearer to the author's intent.

A film is made up of still images flashed in rapid succession to simulate movement. If you take a movie and slow it down to view the film frame by frame, each one becomes unconnected and you lose track of the action. The same is true of reading. You need a good speed to appreciate the meaning. When a person reads slowly and word by word, like frame by frame, they are not reading on the level of ideas and meaning unravels.

The power of review

If you are to remember what you read, it is vital to review the information. Pioneering experimental psychologist Herman Ebbinghaus devised the curve of forgetting over time. In his paper, 'Über das Gedächtnis' ('On Memory', later translated as 'Memory: a Contribution to Experimental Psychology') published in 1885, he showed that as more time elapses after learning more information is forgotten. Ebbinghaus's original research concentrated on learning nonsense syllables in an attempt to rid his stimuli of conventional meaning that would bias the results. This approach has been criticised by more recent researchers in the field of memory but the overall notion of forgetting rapidly after a learning period still holds true.

His findings reveal that the best performance of recall occurs soon after the learning has taken place. However, if you do nothing with the material after a period of study or reading, you forget 80 per cent of the detail within 24 hours. This is a shocking statistic, which means that unless you put in place a review schedule you are wasting 48 minutes of every hour spent reading. If you do nothing for a month you needn't have bothered reading at all as you will typically remember about 4 per cent. I will cover reviewing in more detail in the chapter on studying (Chapter 9).

Using images and imagination

According to Edgar Dale's research in the late 1960s, we remember approximately 10 per cent of what we read compared with 30 per cent of what we see and up to 90 per cent of what we do.

'I hear and I forget. I see and I remember. I do and I understand.'

Chinese proverb often attributed to Confucius

This sounds like bad news for learning by reading. Are you doomed to forget almost everything that you read? Actually, this is not the case. If you can visualise information as you read and imagine yourself in the action, the brain will treat this exactly the same as a real experience and store it in such a way that you will have near perfect recall. Some authors are very skilled at painting word pictures and you can vividly imagine characters and scenes. Have you ever read a book and then gone to see a film adaptation only to be disappointed that the characters do not look like you had imagined them?

Professor Stephen Hawking from Cambridge University is one of the world's leading theoretical physicists. He suffers from motor neurone disease, a disorder that causes muscle weakness and atrophy throughout the body caused by degeneration of the

nerve cells that control muscles. Hawking says, ' … it was difficult for me to write things down so I tended to think in pictures
and diagrams that I could visualise in my head.'

 'Imagination is more important than knowledge. For
knowledge is limited, whereas imagination embraces
the entire world, stimulating progress, giving birth to
evolution.'

Albert Einstein

If you are reading a study book, pay particular attention to
graphs, charts and diagrams. Try to imagine pictorial representations or analogies. As described by Hawking, it is possible to
represent very complex systems by visual representations.

Subvocalisation for comprehension and memory

In Chapter 2 I briefly mentioned that subvocalisation, or
'hearing the word' in your head, is often wrongly labelled as
counterproductive in speed reading. Many courses advocate that
students attempt to eliminate it entirely. If you have ever tried
to stop yourself subvocalising you will probably have noticed a
steep decline in comprehension.

According to the *Guinness Book of Records*, the fastest speaker
in the world, Sean Shannon from Canada, is able to talk at 655
words per minute. To put this into context he is able to deliver
Hamlet's 'To be or not to be …' soliloquy in 23.8 seconds.
Speech speed is limited by the physical movement of the tongue,
mouth and vocal chords so you can think far faster than you
can speak. Speeds of 1,000wpm can easily be subvocalised so it
clearly doesn't slow you down. Hearing the words in your head
greatly improves comprehension. One of the really great aspects
of being conscious of subvocalisation is that you can manipulate

it to your advantage. Experiment varying the volume, like the control knob on your stereo. Try turning the volume down a little so that you can still hear the words but more softly at the back of your mind. When you read something important turn the volume right up so you are shouting the words in your head. This makes them really stand out in your memory. If you have met the author or heard them speak, it is interesting to imagine them reading their book. This is more engaging reading and you will recognise their turn of phrase and intonation which can greatly improve your enjoyment and understanding of a book. Think of Alan Bennett, for example, reading one of his monologues in his distinctive Yorkshire accent.

STOP YOUR TIMER NOW (word count 1,687)

Comprehension questions

1   You read words letter by letter. True or False? [1]

2   The word 'of' is described as what kind of word? [1]

3   When should you look up unfamiliar words in a dictionary? [1]

4   According to Herman Ebbinghaus, how much detail is forgotten within 24 hours of learning? [1]

5   According to Edgar Dale, what percentage of what we read, see and do is remembered? [3]

6   How can you increase the amount that you recall from reading? [1]

7   Subvocalisation slows you down. True or False? [1]

8   How can you use subvocalisation to your advantage to recall salient parts of a piece of text? [1]

Check your answers in Appendix 1.

Number of points × 10 = % comprehension

Calculation

Timer reading

    Minutes:

    Seconds: divide by 60 and add to whole minutes

1,687/time =   Speed (words per minute)

Enter your comprehension and speed in the chart in the Introduction.

CHAPTER 9

Reading for study

START YOUR TIMER NOW

'Books are the carriers of civilisation.
Without books, history is silent,
literature dumb, science crippled,
thought and speculation at a standstill.'

Henry David Thoreau (1817–1862)

Studying is one of the main reasons for reading, yet it is one of the least understood aspects of the activity. In many schools, colleges and even universities children and young adults are told to study but with little or no information on how to do so effectively. They rely on the reading techniques that they learnt when they were in primary school. Their note-taking techniques are ad hoc at best. It is therefore little wonder that so many students struggle to revise effectively and are terrified when it comes to exams. In this chapter I shed some light on how to approach a textbook, take effective notes and then remember the important information long term.

How to approach a textbook

We saw in Chapter 6 how you can get an overview of a book by skimming or scanning the text. This is especially useful when studying. To get the most from a textbook it needs to be integrated to your existing knowledge and to be retained afterwards.

The following process will help you to tackle a textbook in a fraction of the usual time.

1 Preparation

As Stephen Covey said in his book *The Seven Habits of Highly Effective People*, 'Begin with the end in mind'.

Before tackling the book it is important to set your objectives and define goals. Break your goals into smaller aims. How long do you want to work for per session and how much do you want to cover? Ask yourself why you are reading the book. What specific questions do you want to answer? Asking questions before you begin enables your subconscious to go to work as soon as you open the book. You will be on the lookout for particular facts and will be more likely to spot relevant information. Often the answers will seem to leap out at you. Spend five minutes jotting down (or Mind Mapping) what you already know about the subject. This gets you in the right state of mind to engage with the book, boosts concentration and means that you will lay a firm foundation to build upon. Connecting new and existing knowledge is far more effective than trying to acquire information in isolation.

2 Overview

Go through the whole book very quickly. Pay particular attention to summaries, conclusions, illustrations, diagrams, graphs and headings. Look at the contents page and index. Try to understand how the book or document is organised and discover its structure and format.

You can read a text in a similar way to how you would approach a newspaper. Newspapers and study books are divided into sections. You only read the sports section if you're interested in sports and the business pages for business. Even then, you don't read all the sports news or all the business stories. Newspaper headlines (like section or chapter headings) give a good indication of what the story is about, usually with a summary in the first paragraph.

A good approach is to tear up lots of strips of paper to act as bookmarks so you can quickly return to points of interest. Remember, you are not aiming to read sections at this point, just to identify where the key information is located. Imagine you are attempting to complete a jigsaw puzzle. This part is analogous to studying the picture on the front of the box and spreading out the pieces.

3 Gather information

'Skim and dip' through the book. Don't be tempted to dwell too long on any one section. Make notes as you read (building up a Mind Map is a good tool for this). Be selective in your reading. Remember your questions. Most information tends to be concentrated at the beginning and end of chapters so pay particular attention to these.

Start with a sketchy overview and refine it bit by bit as you assimilate more information.

 'My reading technique is actually comprehension by accumulation.'

Evelyn Wood

4 Skip difficult bits

If there are parts of the text that you struggle with, just jump over them and read on. The more context you have, the easier these parts will become. Getting bogged down in detail does not serve any useful purpose. Returning to our jigsaw analogy, the more pieces you put in place, the easier it is to see where the remaining parts fit in.

5 Draw things together and review

The final stage is to tie things together. Return to noteworthy parts of the text, fill in any gaps and answer your questions. If you want to retain what you have learnt from the book, as we will see below, you have to review. Remember to celebrate. This may sound frivolous but it is very important. It associates study with reward and motivates you next time you have a similar situation. The whole time you are enjoying yourself your subconscious is assimilating, integrating and interpreting what you have learnt so that it is embedded at a deeper level.

 **brilliant timesaver**

With the above technique you can get a good summary of a book in about an hour, depending on length and required level of detail. However, you can easily increase this fivefold. All you do is recruit four like-minded friends. You each select a book, study it using the above technique and end up with a Mind Map summary. You photocopy the Mind Maps so that you each have a copy or, if using a computer, you can easily share the files. Each person in turn gives a short presentation to the group about their text as the others add to and personalise the relevant Mind Map. Assuming that it takes an hour to study the material and 20 minutes for each presentation, in less than three hours everyone in the group has a basic understanding of five books. This is extremely useful for 'reading around' a university subject or even broadening knowledge in general. Once again, you need to *review* the Mind Maps to retain the learning.

When studying for an exam it is vital that you not only comprehend and understand what you read but also are able to retain and recall relevant information. The key to doing so is taking succinct and easily memorised notes. Memory and understanding rely on imagination, association and patterns. A technique such as Mind Mapping makes use of this and works in harmony with the brain rather than trying to restrict it to just linear notes.

 **example**

'I first met Phil a few years ago in an effort to remember the plethora of case law required for my legal studies. Whilst my Mind Mapping skills insofar as drawing were poor (they still are), I understood them, which is all that counts. After a short while I was at the point where my study notes for complex subjects were reduced to drawings on cards. I am pleased to say that I received unprecedented grades. From a work perspective, I need to continually study, and remember cases. Try researching Section 6 of the Consumer Credit Act 1974, and you will see why this system of remembering exceeds traditional methods. You just need to take that leap of faith, and discard "ye old faithful" linear notes.'

Tony Bukhari

How to Mind Map

Mind Mapping, devised in the 1970s by Tony Buzan, enables you to summarise the contents of a study book on a single page. This helps you see everything in context and revise more easily. If you need to take notes at a more detailed level you can speed read and Mind Map a book chapter by chapter.

The process applies the following rules:

1 **Start in the centre of an A3 or larger blank page in landscape orientation** (long edge across the top and bottom). Starting in the centre gives your brain freedom to spread out in all directions and to express itself more freely and naturally.

2 **Draw an image or picture in the centre of the paper representing the topic or subject being considered.** Images promote creativity and imagination. A central image is more interesting, keeps you focused, helps you concentrate, and gives your brain more stimulation.

3 **Use colours throughout.** Colours are as stimulating to your brain, as are images. Colour adds extra vibrancy and life to your Mind Map. Using a common colour for related ideas ties them together and creates greater clarity of thought.

4 **Draw tree-like branches radiating out from, and connected to, the central image.** These 'main branches' form the categories of your thinking. In terms of a book these would be the chapter headings.

5 **Connect your main branches to second and third level branches like the twigs of a tree.** Your brain works by association. Connecting your main and sub-level branches creates and establishes an architecture for your thoughts. This network of associations promotes understanding and memory.

6 **Make your branches curved rather than straight-lined.** Using curved, organic-looking branches adds visual variety and are far more attractive to your eye.

7 **Write one keyword or draw an image on each branch.** Single keywords give your Mind Map more power and flexibility. Each single word or image is like a multiplier, generating its own special array of associations and connections. When you use single key words, each one is freer and therefore better able to spark off new ideas and new thoughts. Phrases or sentences tend to dampen this triggering effect.

8 **Use images throughout.** Images stimulate creativity and aid memory so it makes sense to use these as liberally as possible.

9 **Link related ideas on different parts of the Map with arrows**. Insights are often made by connecting ideas that had previously been separated across different pages. A Mind Map allows you to see these relationships and represent them visually by arrows. If there are multiple connections making the use of arrows confusing, you can add icons to related branches to signify connections.

You can find out more details about Mind Mapping in Tony Buzan's books, listed in Further reading.

As well as effectively taking notes from books, Mind Mapping can be used for organising your thoughts prior to any other form of communication. In fact, I used a series of Mind Maps to help me plan and structure this book (Figure 9.1).

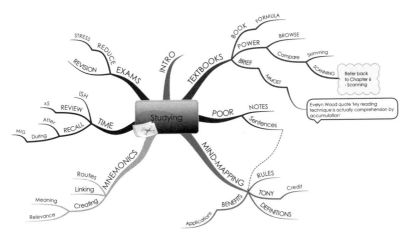

Figure 9.1 A Mind Map plan of this chapter

There are a myriad of Mind Mapping software packages that, to a greater or lesser extent, comply with the rules above. I use (and teach) iMindMap. This is the only software I have found that follows all the laws. See Useful websites in Further reading for more details.

 **example**

I did a series of one-to-one coaching sessions with a GCSE student who was struggling with her revision, especially in Science. I taught her Mind Mapping, some memory techniques and a very basic introduction to speed reading. Her teachers had previously predicted that she would get a mixture of Bs and Cs. In her final exams she got one A* and the rest were all Bs. She now uses Mind Mapping as a matter of course in her A-level studies.

Mnemonics

If you forget most of what you read there is little point in reading at all. Certainly when studying, it is vital to remember the important points and key facts. This can be achieved with the aid of memory techniques, called mnemonics.

Most mnemonics work by imposing some kind of meaning or significance on largely unexciting data or information. The brain craves stimulation and when confronted with dry data it will mostly instantly forget it. If, on the other hand, the brain receives lots of stimulation from an interesting experience it will store this much more firmly. It is logical that low stimulation (data) leads to less possible neuronal connections in the brain whereas experiences with all the senses leads to high stimulation and hence more potential connections.

The key is to represent data in a format closer to experience. As mentioned in Chapter 8, imagining pictures (and involving other senses) is an important aspect of memory. The brain stores vividly imagined experiences in the same way as real life events. One of the simplest but most powerful mnemonics is the Link System. This works by taking each element in a list and connecting it to the next in a dreamlike story. You form a chain of associations or links, hence the name. It is important that the connections have some logic to them (though this can sometimes be a little tenuous) and that each element is a physical object, person or animal that can be assigned a colour, smell, taste, sound or movement.

The following eight principles are useful to keep in mind when creating links as they strengthen connections. To help you remember them, they spell out the acronym SEAHORSE. Fittingly, the area in the brain that plays a key role in consolidating new memories, the hippocampus, is so called because of its seahorse-like shape ('hippocampus' is Latin for 'seahorse').

Senses

When an author uses rich, sensual descriptions, stories come to life. The same is true of memories. Using a 'multi-sensory' approach, involving as many of your senses as you can, makes the memory much stronger and easier to recall. It is usually best to include positive or pleasurable sensations and avoid negative or repulsive ones.

Exaggeration

By accentuating sensations to make them larger, louder, more scented, sweeter, sourer and more tactile you can boost what you remember. The brain filters out the mundane and ordinary. Exaggeration makes things extraordinary.

Action

Create imaged situations with as much action as possible. Dramatic action scenes in novels are memorable. Imagined scenes representing non-fiction concepts are no different. Memories will be even stronger if you are involved and engaged in the action rather than a bystander simply observing. Try to think of a reason why the things are happening. Make the story flow.

Humour

Play with the most absurd, surreal, off-the-wall ideas that spring to mind. Things that make you smile, giggle or groan, even bad jokes and puns, will increase your enjoyment of learning and therefore increase your memory.

Order

Ordered items are easier to recall than those that are jumbled up. Take great care to link each item in sequence once rather than allow yourself to return to an object already covered. This strict ordering will prevent you from missing out objects by jumping ahead.

Repetition

Repetition boosts what you can remember. Every time you return and do a review of the information it reinforces the memory, making it easier to recall the content of a book. We will examine this a little more closely when we consider 'the ideal study hour', shortly.

Symbols

Study books are often concerned with abstract concepts. These do not lend themselves to sensual, actively imagined scenes. This problem can be solved by symbolism. Represent the concept with an object that symbolises it. This can be based on the sound of the word, or the meaning. For example, time could be represented by a pocket watch, electrical current by a currant bun and pressure by a bicycle pump.

Enjoy

Using your memory and your imagination to learn should be easy and fun. If you can make it fun to do, you will want to keep doing it. A well-trained imagination will help make memorising a delight.

The Method of Loci

One of the disadvantages of the Link System is that if you miss a connection the chain breaks and is very difficult continue. Help is at hand in the form of the Mental Journey, also called the Roman Room, Memory Palace or Method of Loci.

This was devised in Ancient Greece by orators to enable them to make long speeches. Written notes were a prohibitively expensive technology simply to be used once. The Romans later adopted the technique.

'The first notion is placed in the forecourt: the second in the atrium: the remainder are committed not just to bedrooms and parlours but to statues and the like … This done, when it is required to revive the memory one begins from the first place to run through all, demanding what has been entrusted to them, of which one will be reminded by the image.'

Quintilian, a Roman teacher of rhetoric (AD $c.35$–$c.100$)

The system works by preselecting a well-known journey. This could be a tour through the rooms of your house, a trip from home to the local shops or your journey to work. Dominic O'Brien, eight times World Memory Champion, sometimes uses golf courses. At each location along the journey imagine a person or object that symbolises each fact or concept from a book. As you retrace your steps in your imagination you will encounter the objects again and hence recall the information. If you forget one of the objects you can simply move to the next location and try to fill in the gap later.

Making the best use of your study time

Recall during learning

How long do you read and make notes without a break whilst studying? Do you plod on for hours on end until the exhaustion or boredom becomes unbearable? It is a commonly held myth that in order to learn something you have to hit the books for hours and hours until you have drilled it into your head.

Do you find yourself daydreaming when you should be working? As the pace of life gets faster we feel we have to work harder and harder. This leads to stress, burnout and ineffectiveness. Daydreaming is our natural release from this.

Psychologists call the diminishing returns from extended periods of study the 'recall during learning curve'. We naturally remember more from the start of a learning session (the primacy effect) and a reasonable amount from the end (the recency effect). However, the middle third is almost a waste of time (Figure 9.2).

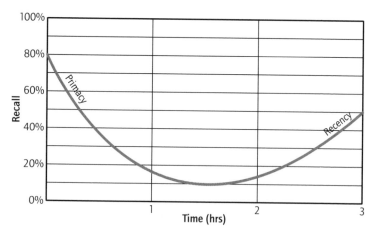

Figure 9.2 Recall during learning curve

You can boost the recall of important information by associating or repeating things. Many students use repetition as a brute-force method of memorising information. This can be used more effectively as will be explained later when considering reviews. In addition, anything that is out of the ordinary or different from the rest stands out in your memory. This is called the von Restorff effect, after Hedwig von Restorff, the German psychologist who first identified it in 1933 (Figure 9.3).

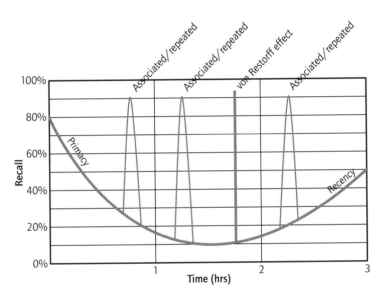

Figure 9.3 Recall during learning curve plus associated/repeated items and von Restorff effect

The best way to learn is little and often. Work for a while, then when your brain starts to daydream, wander, drift away, or get bored – stop – take a break and then start learning again. You can actually remember much more from a period of reading if you break it down into little chunks than if you do it all in one go. Each time you break you create a new primacy and a new recency so you can recall more by working less. The new graph is shown in Figure 9.4 overleaf.

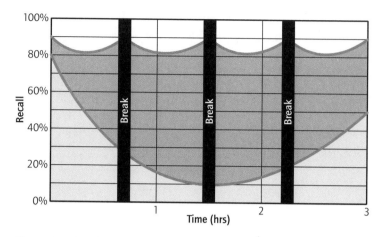

Figure 9.4 Recall during learning curve with breaks

Recall after learning

As we saw in Chapter 8, if you do nothing after a learning period your memory drops off frighteningly rapidly and you forget 80 per cent of the detail within 24 hours.

How do we solve this problem? Typically recall rises a short while after studying, when the brain has had a chance to absorb and organise the new information. After a break of about 10 minutes following a one-hour learning or reading period, spend a short time revising the material covered. The next day review the material again. Then review after one week, one month and finally three months. This should suffice to lodge the information in your long-term memory. Using Mind Maps for note-taking greatly reduces the amount of time required to complete a review. For example, a Mind Map of an entire chapter of a book that may have taken an hour to complete can be reviewed in 90 seconds (Figure 9.5).

Figure 9.5 Recall hand

The ideal study hour

The ideal study hour combines breaks and reviews into a coherent whole that can be followed easily.

An hour is broken down into blocks of time as follows:

- 5 minutes of mental preparation. It makes sense to be in the right state of mind for learning. Do some gentle physical exercise to get better blood and oxygen flow to the brain. You start off awake and alert, ready to take in information.

- 20 minutes' reading and taking notes. This step is acquiring new information.

- 5 minute break. The body is about 90 per cent water by volume so grab a drink (ideally water) in this break. It is always important to get up and move around during breaks. If you stay at your desk thinking about what you have learnt this is not a true break. Don't feel guilty about frequent breaks. They are vitally important, not only to keep yourself alert, but to allow your subconscious to integrate the new material.

- 15 minutes' reviewing the notes that you made yesterday, one week ago, one month and three months ago. This won't take long, especially if you use Mind Maps to condense and summarise information.

- 5 minute break. Practise relaxation techniques to be better prepared for exams or listen to music (see Chapter 4).

- 10 minutes' reviewing. Because we recall more from the end of a session than from the middle, the last 10 minutes of the hour is the ideal time for reviewing and completing the new work studied earlier. At this point you will see any gaps, additional connections or parts you do not yet understand.

- If you are working for two hours and you have completed all your reviews during the first hour scheme, just repeat the process but spend the 15-minute block studying new material and review both this and the 20-minute session in the final 10 minutes.

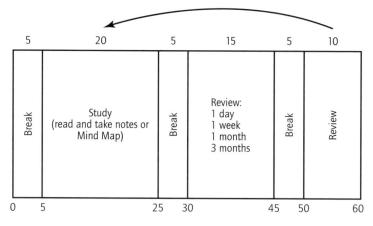

Figure 9.6 Study hour grid

 **example**

'As I started the pursuit of the Chartered Institute of Public Finance and Accountancy (CIPFA) professional accountancy qualification, I knew that striking an effective work–life balance was going to be challenging. However, I had no inclination that the future course of events was going to be dominated by one subject – Accounting for Decision Making (ADM).

I sat ADM four times prior to June 2006. During that period, I experienced difficulties when trying to read the syllabus material quickly. It was especially difficult around the time of revision, with a large volume of material to be covered several times. An analysis of my exam study skills revealed that there was room for improvement.

As a result, when I saw the speed reading course advertised by CIPFA I quickly booked up to attend. My main reason for enrolling was to gain the ability to read large volumes of information quickly while increasing my understanding of that information.

During the speed reading course, I went through a number of practical exercises aimed at measuring my performance in this area. From the chart plotted by the tutor for these exercises, I had achieved an increase in my reading speed as well as the level of comprehension of the information read. Thus I achieved my objective for attending the course and at that time I hoped that this would help me with my exam.

Towards the end of the course, I was extremely happy to note that Mind Mapping was going to be taught. In the past, CIPFA tutors suggested that Mind Mapping would be a useful exam technique for revision.

I utilised 'the ideal study hour' technique, which I used daily. This helped me to store information in my long-term memory, while reviewing information regularly, which was essential for my exam. I also took regular breaks, which I had not done previously during the revision stage.

I utilised the Mind Mapping techniques to Mind Map the 20 chapters of the ADM syllabus. I then drew individual Mind Maps of these chapters, which I reviewed regularly, especially during my revision preparation.

Two weeks before the exam, I reviewed Mind Maps regularly, adhering to 'the ideal study hour', and ensuring that I got plenty of sleep and relaxation.

During the exam, I was able to read the questions quickly and comprehend what was required easily which helped in the selection of four questions   ▶

to complete. This reading and comprehension proved crucial in the latter part of the exam. Essentially, I was running out of time and I had to choose one out of two questions. My speed reading skills helped me to reread these questions quickly and the preparation done using the Mind Mapping techniques helped me to choose the one that was less time-consuming to complete in the remaining exam time.

Due to the time and effort that I put into my revision preparation, the support I received from my workplace and my knowledge of ADM, I expected to pass ADM. However, with the addition of the speed reading and Mind Mapping skills as well as the preparation of various lists relating to possible exam questions, this enhanced my chances of passing ADM. Now that I have passed ADM, I have achieved the CIPFA Professional Accountancy Qualification (PAQ) Diploma, resulting in my being recognised as a part-qualified Accountant.

Finally, in order to obtain the full Professional Accountancy Qualification, I need to complete two additional modules. I will continue to use the speed reading and Mind Mapping skills during my preparation for the final exam to enhance my chances of being successful in achieving the CIPFA PAQ.'

St Claire Thornhill

STOP YOUR TIMER NOW (word count 4,426)

Comprehension questions

1 Why should you pose questions before reading a textbook? [1]

2 Where is most information located in a textbook? [1]

3 What should you do if you come across difficult parts of a book? [1]

4 Why start a Mind Map with an image rather than a word? [1]

5 Why is exaggeration important in forming strong memories? [1]

6 What potential problem with the Link System does the Method of Loci overcome? [1]

7 All other things being equal, which two parts of a learning period do you remember most strongly? [2]

8 How many reviews do you need to transfer information to your long-term memory? [1]

9 How much of a one-hour study session is spent covering new material? [1]

Check your answers in Appendix 1.

Number of points × 10 = % comprehension

Calculation
Timer reading
    Minutes:
    Seconds: divide by 60 and add to whole minutes

4,426/time =   speed (words per minute)

Enter your comprehension and speed in the chart in the Introduction.

CHAPTER 10

Reading from computer screens

START YOUR TIMER NOW

'A capacity, and taste, for reading, gives access to whatever has already been discovered by others. It is the key, or one of the keys, to the already solved problems. And not only so. It gives a relish, and facility, for successfully pursuing the [yet] unsolved ones.'

Abraham Lincoln

Although I have been talking about use of digital devices and reading from Kindles, iPads and the like throughout the book, there are some specific issues, especially when working at a computer screen, that are worth considering.

This chapter will examine two of the biggest drains on most people's time: email and reading from the web.

One of the greatest benefits of using a computer is that you can modify how text is presented. This offers huge scope for experimentation with colour, fonts and line spacing. This is largely down to personal preference but I will try to introduce a little science into the process.

I will describe how your work environment needs to be managed for optimum reading from a screen, especially office lighting and the position and angle of your monitor.

When working from a screen it is very important to take regular breaks and change the focus of your eyes so I will cover techniques to help rest and refresh the eyes.

I will also return to the topic of guiding with screens in mind.

Email

Are you a slave to email? Do you feel the need to check your BlackBerry or smart phone at every spare opportunity? Do you have your computer ring a bell or beep to announce every incoming message? Do you spend the first hour at work checking and replying to emails? Just because modern communication makes it possible to reply instantaneously, it is not necessarily the best strategy. Certainly, if you are reading, you don't want to be interrupted by emails. Set aside your reading time and close down your email app and web browser, switch off your phone and close the door to your office or study. You will be far more focused, efficient and the email will wait.

How often have you been busy all day but when you look back, have not actually achieved anything substantial?

A 1999 study by Gallup for Pitney Bowes Inc. ('Messaging Practices in the Knowledge Economy') showed that the average UK worker sends and receives on average 171 messages a day and is interrupted every ten minutes. This is disastrous for productivity. There are four types of email:

● unsolicited spam, most of which can be filtered out automatically;

● newsletters, ezines, Facebook groups, etc which you subscribe to and sometimes give you value but are mostly time-wasting. They often don't need to be read and certainly don't need to be replied to;

- emails that are non-urgent, demand a response but are not really as important as they purport to be. These would not have serious consequences if ignored;

- finally, genuinely important emails that you do need to respond to.

The final category are in the minority and as they are important usually deserve a reasoned response rather than a knee-jerk reaction. If you set aside a specific time each day devoted to answering these important emails, you will be able to focus on one thing at a time without constant interruptions, achieve what you set out to do and have more time for meaningful work.

Websites

American sociologist and IT pioneer Ted Nelson coined the term 'hypertext' in 1963, meaning a series of documents that link together. Sir Tim Berners-Lee, whilst working at the CERN laboratories in Geneva, took the concept further and initiated a project aimed at facilitating sharing information among researchers. In 1990 the first successful communication between a Hypertext Transfer Protocol (HTTP) client and server via the internet took place. This was the birth of the World Wide Web. The first website went online in 1991 and, on 30 April 1993, CERN announced that the World Wide Web would be free to anyone. Google now estimate that there are over a trillion web pages.

The explosion of the web can be seen as the biggest advance in information dissemination since Gutenberg's invention of the printing press about 1448. With all this information available it is impossible to read even a tiny fraction. It is very easy to get drawn into following links when using the web. Hypertext is a totally new form of reading where a single document can link to literally hundreds of others through multiple levels. Whilst this is a very useful tool for research, it can be very time-consuming and even counterproductive.

'Rapidly finding, evaluating, using, and communicating information will become central instructional issues. Highly literate individuals will be able to skim web pages, link to other web pages, and generally sift through large amounts of information in a short time. Individuals who read slowly and haltingly will still be evaluating the first screen of information by the time a more rapid reader has already completed the informational task. In a world of vast information resources, literacy will be defined around the rate at which one can read, write, comprehend and communicate information.'

Dr Cynthia Doss, *Journal of Language Studies* (2010) 6:1

As I have already mentioned on several occasions, the key aspect of effective reading is being selective in what you read, to get the information you need and moving on.

Lighting for screens

It is especially important to have correct illumination when reading from a computer screen or mobile device such as a Kindle, iPad or smart phone. Lighting should be even, clear and soft to avoid glare. Natural daylight is best but if this is not possible use a light specifically designed for reading. A traditional incandescent bulb, no longer manufactured due to its poor energy efficiency, gives off a yellowish light. Energy-saving fluorescent light bulbs tend to give a cold, bluish light although newer designs are improving this. I would recommend full spectrum halogen light bulbs that burn brighter, whiter and hotter than other bulbs and are much closer to daylight.

Avoid fluorescent tubes, often used in offices, as these produce a flicker that can have detrimental effects. These include migraines, drowsiness, general stress, and an adverse effect on mood.

Experiment with different levels of illumination to get the best clarity of text. If the light level in your office or work area varies then you should vary the brightness and contrast of your screen accordingly.

Modification of text

If you are reading a document on a word processing package such as Apple Pages or Microsoft Word, you can change the settings to make text easier to read.

Colour

Research by the Colour Usage Research Lab at NASA Ames Research Centre states that to maximise legibility, the prime consideration for colour choice is a measure called 'Luminance Contrast'. Whilst the science of colour perception is very complex, the main issue is that individual colours have different perceived brightness or luminance values. The greater the difference between the luminance of the background colour and that of the text, the greater the contrast. Higher contrast generally leads to clearer and more legible text. The greatest contrast is traditional black text on a white background (or white on black). However, some people find this too harsh so prefer to go for an alternative. Colour (and hence luminance) can be defined by three values: hue, saturation and lightness; 100 per cent lightness is white and 0 per cent lightness is black. If we set lightness at the neutral level of 50 per cent and ignore saturation by setting it at 100 per cent, the following table gives the relative luminance values of different hues:

Red	54%
Orange	65%
Yellow	93%
Green	80%
Cyan	87%

Blue   44%

Magenta 70%

Notice that blue has the lowest value. NASA gives the following advice on use of blue:

'Pure blue should not be used for fine detail or background … Blue has low luminance … the blue primary stimulates mostly the short-wave cones, which contribute little to the visual process that forms edges (like those that make up letters). Thus any graphics that differ from the background only in the blue primary will be hard to read.'

A solution is offered of using blue text against a high luminance colour, such as white or yellow, or using pale blue on black.

Popular combinations include green, yellow or orange on a black background or blue on a white background. Using the table above, choose colour combinations that differ widely in luminance and experiment with what feels easiest and most comfortable to read.

Font

There is a great deal of debate on the effect that fonts can have on the ease of reading from a screen. In 1996 Microsoft released a font called Verdana that was designed to be easy to read at small sizes on computer screens. However, the effectiveness of this has been disputed by some researchers. One of the most contentious issues is whether fonts with serifs (like Times) are more or less readable than those without, sans serif (like Verdana, Helvetica and Arial). For online reading, sans serif fonts seem easier on the eyes. One possible reason is that on-screen, the resolution generally isn't good enough to display crisp serifs. This results in letters being a little more blurry and slightly less recognisable. Printed text tends to be more legible with serifs. It is believed that serifs serve as 'horizontal cues' that guide the eye along a line of text. Of course, using a physical guide negates this as it will have a far bigger effect. Once again, experiment with different fonts to decide which work best for you. I like 'Helvetica Neue Light' for both online and printed material.

Line spacing

Inter-line spacing within a paragraph can also have an impact on readability. This should be sufficiently large so that the lines of text don't start blurring together. The 1.5 space option seems to work best but once again this is down to personal preference.

Guiding with screens

As mentioned in Chapter 7, you are still able to guide your eyes when using a computer screen. You can use a pen, knitting needle or chopstick as a guide just as you would with printed media. The only difference being that you need to hold this a short distance in front of the screen to avoid scratching it or accidentally turning pages on a touch screen device. If you find this uncomfortable you can use the computer's mouse pointer as a guide. This can be controlled with a mouse, track pad or, more closely analogous to a physical guide, with a stylus on a graphics tablet.

Viewing angle

It is important to have a comfortable viewing angle for your screen. Make sure that the monitor is directly in front of you so that you don't have to turn your head to read. Also, make sure that it is at the correct height so that your neck is free and not under any strain. You can buy monitor stands or, if only a slight adjustment is needed, you can place a book underneath the base.

Take care that your screen is sufficiently far away that you can make use of your peripheral vision. As explained in Chapter 5, this is about 50 cm from your eyes. Laptop keyboards sometimes make it a little difficult to position the screen sufficiently far away whilst still being able to reach the keyboard with ease. If this is the case, it may be worth investing in a flat screen monitor and separate keyboard for your office or study. These are now relatively inexpensive. If you are using an iPad for your reading, the cover can be folded to stand it upright at an appropriate distance.

Looking after your eyes

The UK Health and Safety Executive states, in relation to the Health and Safety (Display Screen Equipment) Regulations 1992, Regulation 4:

'Every employer shall so plan the activities of users at work in his undertaking that their daily work on display screen equipment is periodically interrupted by such breaks or changes of activity as reduce their workload at that equipment.'

The guidance specifies:

'Whenever possible, jobs at display screens should be designed to consist of a mix of screen-based and non screen-based work to prevent fatigue and to vary visual and mental demands. Where the job unavoidably contains spells of intensive display screen work (whether using the keyboard or input device, reading the screen, or a mixture of the two), these should be broken up by periods of non-intensive, non-display screen work. Where work cannot be so organised, e.g. in jobs requiring only data or text entry requiring sustained attention and concentration, deliberate breaks or pauses must be introduced … if the display screen work is visually demanding any activities during breaks should be of a different visual character. Breaks must also allow users to vary their posture. Exercise routines which include blinking, stretching and focusing eyes on distant objects can be helpful and could be covered in training programmes.'

I would recommend that you look out of the window or focus on the distance, as much as possible, approximately every 15 to 20 minutes when reading from a screen.

The muscles of your eyes, just like those in the other parts of your body, need to have time to rest and relax. This is especially true if you have been reading for a long while or focusing on a screen.

STOP YOUR TIMER NOW (word count 2,238)

Comprehension questions

1   What do I advocate doing with important emails? [1]

2   If natural daylight is not available, what is the best alternative illumination source for computer screens? [1]

3   What factor determines a clearly readable colour scheme? [1]

4   When reading from a computer screen is it better to use a font with or without serifs? [1]

5   What line spacing is suggested? [1]

6   You cannot use a physical guide with a computer screen. True or False? [1]

7   What distance from your eyes is optimal to position a screen? [1]

8   Name two exercises during breaks advocated by the UK Health and Safety Executive. [2]

9   How often should you break or refocus when working at a computer screen? [1]

Check your answers in Appendix 1.

Number of points $\times$ 10 = % comprehension

Calculation

Timer reading

  Minutes:

  Seconds: divide by 60 and add to whole minutes

2,238/time =   Speed (words per minute)

Enter your comprehension and speed in the chart in the Introduction.

🔍 **brilliant** exercise

The following short exercise will revitalise your eyes and prevent eyestrain.

Rub your hands together briskly, until the palms are quite warm. Lean forward on your elbows and cup your hands over your closed eyes, resting lightly on your face but not touching the eyes themselves. Feel your eyes gently absorb the warmth from your hands and start to relax. Think of blackness; black velvet; a black cat; deep, dark, starless night. Rest like this for at least one minute. Open your eyes and feel refreshed!

This technique is based on the work of alternative therapist and eye-care physician William Horatio Bates (1860–1931). Although most of his more wild claims of being able to improve eyesight without glasses have been debunked by scientists, I believe that eye relaxation is genuinely beneficial.

CHAPTER 11

Improving your vocabulary

START YOUR TIMER NOW

'Not all readers are leaders, but all leaders are readers.'

Harry S. Truman

I n this chapter I will explore an area that often causes readers stress, namely expanding your vocabulary. There is often a mystique associated with this and a feeling that if you haven't had a classical education you are in some way excluded from the intelligentsia. That is nonsense. Building vocabulary relies on structure. Words are broken down into prefixes, roots and suffixes and understanding this leads to knowledge of hundreds or thousands of new words.

By the end of this chapter you will have the keys to unlock a whole new world of possibilities that can transform your enjoyment and appreciation of language.

The English language

It is virtually impossible to give an accurate measure of the number of words in the English language largely because of the imprecise definition of what constitutes a word. A computer analysis of 5,195,769 digitised books conducted in 2010 in a joint Harvard/Google study found the English language to contain 1,022,000 words. The English language is likely to contain the most words of all languages, according to the Oxford English Dictionary, and estimates for the number of words range from one to two million. The language is continually changing, with new words, such as 'omnishambles', becoming accepted every year. Different professions such as medicine, science and computing have their own distinct vocabulary and terminology. According to Professor David Crystal, known chiefly for his research in English language studies and author of around 100 books on the subject, 'Most people know half the words [in a medium-sized dictionary] – about 50,000 – easily. A reasonably educated person about 75,000 and … an ordinary person, one who has not been to university say, would know about 35,000 quite easily'(**http://news.bbc.co.uk/1/hi/ magazine/8013859.stm**). Although 35,000 to 75,000 sounds like a lot, this is probably less than 5 per cent of the total number of words in the language. Although you can often surmise the meaning of a word from its context when reading, a wider vocabulary will improve your comprehension. Command of a large and varied vocabulary is an asset in business, education and social situations.

Many of the words in English originate from Latin or Greek. Words with these origins tend to be formed by combing three components.

At the start of the word is the *prefix*, for example 'iso' meaning 'the same or equal'.

Next comes the *root* of the word. This is the main unit of meaning. For example 'morph' from Greek meaning 'shape or form'.

Finally comes the *suffix* that generally defines characteristics or to which part of speech the word belongs (i.e. adjective, adverb, noun, etc). For example 'ic' meaning 'relating to'.

Therefore the word 'isomorphic' is an adjective meaning 'being of the same or corresponding form' (such as isomorphic crystals).

The *prefix* 'iso' is also used in 'isobaric' meaning 'the same pressure', 'isotopic' meaning 'having the same number of protons' (in a chemical element) or 'isometric' meaning 'having equal dimensions'.

The *root* 'morph' is also used in 'polymorphic', meaning 'having many forms' or 'amorphous', meaning 'without form or shape'.

The *suffix* 'ism' means 'the quality of', so 'isomorphism' is a noun meaning 'the quality of being isomorphic'.

You can see that learning a few basic prefixes, suffixes and roots can open the door to a wealth of new words. The only problem is how to learn these in an easy and fun way. You already know how, from Chapter 9. Simply apply the mnemonic principles defined by the acronym SEAHORSE and link things together. The more imaginative and bizarre the associations the better. Ones that you make up yourself will nearly always be stronger than someone else's. I have included a number to get you started.

Prefixes

In science and mathematics there are standard prefixes that are used to denote powers of ten when used with specific metric units. For example, a kilometre is a thousand metres. This is known as the SI system, short for Système International d'Unités. I have listed the most common prefixes below, with suggested associations.

Note: in computer memory where these terms are also used, because computers work in binary, on-off code, the actual number is the nearest power of two. For example, a kilobyte is 1,024 bytes, not 1,000 as the prefix would suggest.

Tera (T) 100,000,000,0000 – One hundred billion (or trillion). The character Trillian from *The Hitchhikers' Guide to the Galaxy*, screaming in terror at a pterodactyl.

Giga (G) 1,000,000,000 – One billion. Billionaire Bill Gates dancing a jig at a rock concert (gig).

Mega (M) 1,000,000 – One million. Actress Megan Fox in a Virgin Megastore playing *Who Wants to be a Millionaire?*

Kilo (k) 1,000 – One thousand. Imagine a killer running the 1,000 metre race in a stadium and apprehended at the finish line by the police.

Hecto (h) 100 – One hundred. Hector, the bowler-hatted taxman character from the 1990s Inland Revenue advertisements, waving a tax bill for £100.

Deci (d) 0.1 – One tenth. A decimal point separates tenths from units, so deci is 0.1.

Centi (c) 0.01 – One hundredth. A Roman centurion commanding 100 dwarfs (to remind you that it is a hundredth, not a hundred),

Milli (m) 0.001 – One thousandth. The band *The Proclaimers* singing about walking a thousand miles. Duetting with Labour leader, Ed Miliband.

Micro (μ) 0.000001 – One millionth. Looking through a microscope at six microbes swimming in the shape of a number '6' (ten to the power minus six, 10^{-6}).

Nano (n) 0.000000001 – One billionth. An iPod Nano listened to by nine nanas (nano is ten to the power minus nine, 10^{-9}).

Number prefixes

Semi (half) – Think of a semi-detached house (half detached and half connected to the next door house). Semi-skimmed milk, semicircle, semi-skilled work, semi-retired, semitone, semi-final, semiconductor, semi-conscious, semi-derelict.

Demi (half) – Associated with demigod, meaning 'a minor god of half-divine status'. Demi-pension (half board hotel accommodation, from French).

Hemi (half) – Hemisphere (such as half the world). Hemicylindrical (having the shape of half a cylinder, divided lengthways).

Uni (one) – Imagine a unicorn with its single horn. Unicycle, unify, union, unite (make one), unique, unit, universe (meaning the one whole).

Mono (one) – Recall the sinister, black stone monolith in the film *2001: A Space Odyssey.* Monochrome (one colour, typically black and white), monorail, monogamy, monopoly (controlled by one organisation), monotone, monologue.

Bi (two) – Think of the two wheels of a bicycle. Binoculars, binary (having two states: on or off), biennial (happening every two years), bifurcate (to split into two), bifocal glasses, bisexual.

Di (two) – Think of Princess Di and the 'two' other people in her marriage, as she described it, Prince Charles and Camilla. Diatomic (consisting of two atoms), dichotomy (contrast of two opposing views), disyllabic (having two syllables), carbon dioxide.

Duo (two) – Think of a famous duo like Morecambe and Wise, Laurel and Hardy or Batman and Robin (the dynamic duo). Duet, duplex (having two parts), duplicate (double or make a copy).

Tri (three) – Think of a triangle (a shape with three angles); imagine the sound of the musical instrument of the same name. Tricycle, triplets, trefoil (a plant with three-lobed leaves like a shamrock or clover), the Holy Trinity, triathlon, triceps (muscles with three points of attachment), triceratops (three-horned dinosaur), tricolour (a flag with three coloured bands, especially the French flag), tricorne (a three-sided hat).

Tetra (four) – The computer game *Tetris* (all of the blocks in the game are made up of four squares). Tetrahedron (a four-faced solid, i.e. a triangular pyramid), tetrapod (a four-footed animal).

Quadri (four) – A quad bike has four wheels. Quadrangle (a four-sided courtyard), quadratic (an equation with a 'squared' quantity), quadrant (each of the four quarters of a circle), quadruple (increase fourfold), quadriplegia (paralysis of all four limbs), quadruplets (four children from one birth).

Quin (five) – Five babies from one birth are quins (or more properly quintuplets). Quintet (five people playing music together), quintuple (increase fivefold), quincunx (an arrangement of five objects with four forming a square and one in the middle, like '5' on a die).

Penta (five) – The Pentagon – the headquarters of the US Department of Defence is a building with five sides. Pentagram (a five-pointed star), pentathlon (five-event athletic competition), pentachord (a musical instrument with five strings).

Sexa (six) – Think of six sexy people. Sexennial (happening every six years), sextant (an instrument for measuring angles; one sixth of circle, 60 degrees).

Hexa (six) – Think of the six-sided, hexagonal cells of a honeycomb or the Giant's Causeway in Northern Ireland. Hexane (a chemical compound with six carbon atoms), hexapoda (six-legged animals such as insects).

Septem (seven) – September was originally the seventh month before Julius and Augustus Caesar introduced July and August. Septet (seven people playing music or singing together).

Hepta (seven) – Think of Jessica Ennis, the Olympic gold medal-winning heptathlete competing in her seven events. Heptagon (a seven-sided shape), heptarchy (a state containing seven smaller, autonomous regions).

Octa/Octo (eight) – Associate with an eight-armed octopus. Octagon (an eight-sided shape), octave (a series of eight musical notes), October (originally the eight month), octane (a component of petrol with eight carbon atoms).

Nona/Novem (nine) – November was originally the ninth month of the year. Nonagon (a nine-sided shape), nonary (relating to the number nine), Novena (Roman catholic worship over nine days).

Deca/Decem (ten) – Think of the decathlon, and British Olympian Daley Thompson competing in his ten events. Decagon (ten-sided shape), the Decalogue (the Ten Commandments).

General prefixes

Auto – One's own, by oneself, by itself or automatic. Your autobiography is your life story written by yourself. This is a combination of auto –self, bio –life and graph –write. Autocrat (a ruler with absolute power. The word literally means self-power), autograph (a signature, especially of a celebrity), autofocus (a device for automatically focusing a camera).

Contra/Counter – Opposite or against. To contradict someone is to speak 'against' what they are saying. Counteract (act against something to reduce its force), counterfeit (fraudulent imitation, against making something genuine), contravene (to offend against an order or law), contraceptive (a method to prevent conception).

Anti – Also means opposite or against. Take an antisocial person. This is the 'opposite' of being social, or is 'against' being so. Antifreeze (a liquid that acts against water freezing), antidote (a medicine taken to counteract a poison), antonym (a word opposite in meaning), antacid (a medicine that acts against excess stomach acid to neutralise it), antidepressant (a drug that acts against depression).

Hyper – Over, beyond or above. Think of the word hyperactive, which describes a person who is 'overly' active in some way. Hyperventilate (breathe at an abnormally rapid rate), hyperbaric (involving gas at higher than normal pressure), hypersonic (relating to speed greater than five times the speed of sound), hypersensitive, hypertext (see Chapter 10).

Hypo – Under, below. Hypodermic refers to going 'under' the skin, especially relating to an injection, hypothermia (the condition of having abnormally low body temperature), hypomania (a mild form of mania), hypothesis (a proposition made as the basis of reasoning without assumption of its truth; an underlying foundation), hypoxia (deficiency of the amount of oxygen reaching the body's tissues).

Neo – New. Think of Keanu Reeves' character, Neo, in *The Matrix* films discovering his new powers. Neon (an inert gas with atomic number 10; the name means 'something new'), neophobia (an irrational fear of the new or unfamiliar), neolithic (the later part of the Stone Age, also called the New Stone Age), neonatal (relating to newborn babies), neoclassical (relating to the revival of a classical style in art, literature, architecture or music).

Poly – Many, much. Think of lots of parrots! Polyglot (a person who knows or uses many languages), polygon (a many-sided/angled shape), polymer (a molecule built up chiefly or completely from a large number of similar units).

Pro – Motion forwards, favouring or supporting. When you make progress you are stepping 'forward'. If you give the pros in an argument, you are speaking 'for' something by stating its advantages. Promise (to put forward an undertaking or assurance that something will happen), promote (give publicity to or support a product so as to increase sales), proceed/propel (to move forward).

Retro – Denoting action that is directed backwards or reciprocal. Think of retro-style, looking backwards to the 1960s and '70s, typified by hippies. Retrograde (directed or moving backwards, reverting to a former and inferior condition), retrofit (add a component to something that did not have it when manufactured), retrorocket (a small rocket on a spacecraft giving reverse thrust, used to slow it down).

Tele – To or at a distance. Think of watching telly a long distance away (so far you need a telescope to see it). Teleport (transport across space and distance instantly), telekinesis (the supposed ability to move things at a distance through mental power), telematics (the branch of IT which deals with long-distance transmission of information), telephone, telegraph, telegram.

Roots

Aer(o) – Of or relating to air. Think of the chocolate bar that has bubbles of air in it. Aeroplane (a powered, fixed-wing flying vehicle), aeronaut (a traveller in a hot-air balloon, airship or other flying craft), aerosol (a pressurised substance that can be released in a fine spray by means of a propellant gas), aerodynamics (the study of the properties of moving air), aerofoil (a structure of curved surfaces to produce lift in aircraft through the flow of air).

Ann/Enn – Year. In a speech to the Guildhall on 24 November 1992, marking the 40th anniversary of her Accession, Queen Elizabeth II described the closing of the year as an 'annus horribilis', literally 'a horrible year'. Anniversary (the date an event took place in a previous year), annual (occurring once a year), centennial (relating to a 100th anniversary), millennium (a period of 1,000 years), Anno Domini – AD (the year of Our Lord).

Bio – Of or relating to life. Think of 'Baby Bio' plant food promoting stronger growth and more life. Biotechnology (the exploitation of biological processes for industrial or other purposes), biodegradable (an object able to be decomposed by bacteria or other living organisms), biodiversity (the variety of plant and animal life in the world or a particular habitat), biology (the study of life), biopsy (the examination of tissue removed from a living body), biography (a book about someone's life).

Capit – Head. The word capital, the 'head' city of a nation. London is the capital of England. More flippantly, though possibly from the Latin, you wear a cap on your head. Captain (the person in charge of a ship, or leader of a team), decapitate (to cut off the head), per capita (for each person, literally by heads).

Chroma – Colour; of or in colours. Until its discontinuation in 2009, Kodachrome was the oldest surviving brand of colour film. It was introduced by Eastman Kodak in 1935 and used for both still and movie photography. Chromatography (method of separation of a mixture – originally seen as coloured bands), chromakey (replacement of a specific colour in a video image with a separate image), chromogen (a substance that can readily be converted into a dye or coloured compound), chrome (chromium plate, because of the brilliant colours of chromium compounds).

Chrono – Relating to time. Think of a chronometer, an instrument for accurately measuring time, especially in spite of motion or variation in temperature, humidity and air pressure for use in navigation on ships. Chronological (a record of events in terms of the passage of time), chronograph (an instrument for accurately recording time), chronic (an illness persisting for a long time), chronometry (the science of accurate time measurement).

Cycl – Circular. Picture a bicycle, which possesses two 'circles' in the form of its wheels. Unicycle (a single-wheeled cycle), recycle (convert waste into reusable material in a circular process), Cyclops (a member of a race of one-eyed giants), encyclopaedia (books giving all-round education).

Geo – Relating to the earth. Geology is the study of the earth and rocks. Think of a jolly geologist. Geomagnetism (the study of the magnetic properties of the earth), geode (a small cavity in a rock lined with crystals or other mineral matter), geography (study of the physical features of the earth, its atmosphere and human activity).

Graph – Something written, drawn or an instrument that records. Think of someone recording data by drawing a graph. Pictography (an early form of writing using pictorial representations of words or phrases), graphology (the study of handwriting to determine a person's character), pantograph (an instrument for copying a drawing to a different scale using hinged rods), graphite (form of carbon used in pencil leads), polygraph (a machine that detects changes in pulse, breathing, etc used as a lie detector, literally means 'many recordings'), calligraphy (the art of decorative handwriting), photograph (literally 'light drawing'), graphics (visual art or computer images).

Lev – Light in weight. Imagine a magician levitating someone. To make so 'light in weight' that they can float above the ground. Elevate (to raise), levity (to treat a serious matter with humour or with lack of due respect, to make light of).

Man – Hand. Think of a man doing manual work with his hands. Manuscript (a book, document or piece of music written by hand), manufacture (the making of articles on a large scale using machinery, originally the word meant 'made by hand'), and manicure (a cosmetic treatment of the hands, literally 'hand care').

Onym – Name. Someone who does not give their name is anonymous. Synonym (a word or phrase that means exactly the same or nearly the same as another word or phrase in the same language), antonym (a word or phrase that means the opposite of another word or phrase in the same language).

Path – Feeling or disease. A sympathetic person 'feels' the pain of another. Apathy (lack of feeling or enthusiasm), pathological (relating to disease), and sociopath (someone affected by a personality disorder leading to violence with lack of empathy).

Phil – Love. My name, Philip, means lover or fond of horses (hippos is 'horse'). Francophile (a lover of the French), philanthropist (a person or organisation seeking to promote the welfare of others, literally 'mankind-loving'), philosopher (a lover of wisdom).

Phon – Relating to sound. Think of the sound of a phone ringing. Telephone literally means 'sound at a distance'. Phonograph (an early instrument used to record sound using cylinders), phonology (the system of relationships among speech sounds that constitute language), microphone, hydrophone (a microphone that detects sound waves under water), phonics (see Chapter 2).

Photo – Relating to light. Think of a photographer with a very bright flash. Photon (a particle representing a quantum of light), phototherapy (the use of light in the treatment of physical or mental illness), photosynthesis (the process by which green plants use sunlight to synthesise food).

Scrib/Script – Write. Think of a scribe whose job is writing. Transcribe (to put speech or data into written form), describe (to give an account in words with all relevant characteristics, qualities of events), postscript (an additional remark at the end of letter, literally 'later write'), script (the text of a play, film or broadcast), scripture (the writings of a religion).

Son – Relating to sound. A sonic boom, caused by a shockwave from an object travelling faster than the speed of sound, makes a deafening noise. Sonata (a classical composition for an instrumental soloist often with piano accompaniment), sonography (the analysis of sound by graphical representation), sonorous (of a very deep, full voice or other sound).

Therm – Relating to heat. A thermal vest will keep you warm. Thermometer (a device for measuring temperature), thermostat (a device for maintaining constant temperature), isotherm (a line on a map connecting areas of equal temperature), thermodynamics (the branch of physics that deals with the relationship between heat and other forms of energy).

Ver – Truth. To verify is to make sure something is true. Verdict (a decision on an issue of fact in a civil or criminal case), veracity (conformity to facts or accuracy; speaking truly).

Vis/Vid – See, look at. Recall this by the association that vision is someone's ability to 'see'. Video is a moving image, which you 'see' on a screen. Invisible (unable to be seen), provide (to prepare for or foresee), supervisor (someone who observes or oversees another's work).

Suffixes

-able – Capable of. Durable (able to withstand wear, pressure or damage), operable (able to be used), workable (capable of producing the desired effect), indomitable (impossible to subdue).

-arium/-orium – Place for. Auditorium (a place for hearing, a theatre), terrarium (a tank for small land-dwelling animals), aquarium (a tank for fish and water life).

-ess – Female. Lioness, hostess, waitress, actress, shepherdess, stewardess.

-ian – Belonging to (a profession). Musician, librarian, physician, magician, statistician, mathematician, politician.

-metry/-meter – Measurement. Geometry, speedometer, anemometer (a device for measuring wind speed), thermometer.

-ist – One who practises. Physicist, chemist, biologist, optometrist (one who examines eyes and prescribes spectacles), pessimist (one who believes the worst will happen), optimist (one who is hopeful and confident in the future), pragmatist (one who is practical and realistic).

-oid – Like. Android (a robot with human-like appearance), ovoid (more or less egg-shaped), cuboid (cube-like), humanoid (human-like).

-ology – Study or branch of knowledge. Biology, geology, psychology, physiology, sociology, metrology (the study of measurement), meteorology (the study of weather).

-tude – Degree or quantity of. Altitude (height), multitude (a large number or), gratitude (degree of being thankful), fortitude (degree of courage in adversity).

-ward – Direction. Forward, backward, upward, downward, inward, outward, homeward.

If you learn the above prefixes, roots and suffixes, you will be able to understand literally hundreds of new words. I suggest you aim to cover five per day. Where possible, make up your own associations and clearly visualise them. Employ the five reviews as described in Chapter 9. This is only the beginning. There are many more Latin- and Greek-based words. If you Google prefixes, roots and suffixes you will easily find numerous lists to work with.

As I have mentioned previously, you should not stop reading to look up words that you don't know but when you get to the end of a chapter it is a good idea to look back and make a note of unfamiliar words. Find the definitions and build these into your programme of vocabulary building. It is also worth buying a good printed dictionary. Online dictionaries only give you what you search for so are less useful for discovering new words. With a physical dictionary you can start with a prefix and browse to find related words.

If you really want a challenge, you can emulate Dr Yip Swee Chooi from Malaysia who has learnt the 1,774 page *Oxford Advanced Learner English–Chinese Dictionary*. That is 57,000 words and their definitions. Not only does he know every single word, he can tell you the page number and which word it is on that page. For example, the word 'effervescent' is the fifth word on page 463. He doesn't have a photographic memory. He has just used the journey or Loci technique that we covered in Chapter 9. He has come up with 57,000 locations and imagined an image for a word and meaning at each one.

brilliant example

'The ability to read rapidly and retain useful information is paramount in today's world. Think about it … a person's success today is often tied directly to the amount of useful information they know and can use for practical benefit. If you can read faster, you gain a huge competitive advantage in a white-hot competitive world. I've used several techniques to help and enjoy learning more all the time. I find that reading and retaining valuable information is much like physical exercise – if we don't use it, practise with it and continually hone our skills – we lose it. It is imperative   ▶

to continually train our brain and feed it with good quality, market-valuable information. Learning how to read rapidly and retain market-valuable information is imperative for the success-orientated person today. And besides that, it is a lot of fun!'

Terry Brock, MBA, CSP, CPAE, author, professional speaker, former Chief Skype Enterprise Blogger, former AT&T Editor-in-Chief for Networking Exchange Blog

STOP YOUR TIMER NOW (word count 3,968)

Vocabulary questions

Break down each of the following words into their components to determine their meaning. I don't expect you to know all the prefixes, roots and suffixes yet, so you can look back in the chapter when answering these questions.

1 Neophilia

2 Spheroid

3 Geochronologist

4 Polycyclic

5 Controvertible

6 Heptad

7 Whitherward

8 Semicentennial

9 Polyphony

10 Chronophobia

Check your answers in Appendix 1.

Number of points $\times$ 10 = % correct

Calculation

Timer reading

    Minutes:

    Seconds: divide by 60 and add to whole minutes

3,968/time =   Speed (words per minute)

Enter your speed in the chart in the Introduction. As the test is not strictly comprehension you can choose whether to enter this in the chart or not.

CHAPTER 12

Conclusion

'I think books are like people, in the sense that they'll turn up in your life when you most need them.'

Emma Thompson

I do not intend to introduce any new techniques in this chapter but rather to consolidate and summarise those from the previous chapters.

I will return to the questions regarding your beliefs and preconceptions about reading posed in Chapter 1. Hopefully you will have changed your mind about some of these as a result of reading this book. Any journey can suffer minor setbacks along the way so I will tackle some frequently asked questions regarding continued progress and practice. One final note worthy of inclusion is the application of speed reading to alleviate dyslexia and related conditions. I urge you to recommend speed reading to anyone you know with dyslexia as this is not something that sufferers would automatically think of trying. In many cases the techniques can have a very positive impact.

 **recap**

You can remember the main speed reading techniques by the acronym GO FASTER. This stands for:

- **G**uide your eyes
- **O**nly go forwards
- **F**ixate for shorter periods
- **A**ttitude – positive and alert
- **S**tay on the page
- **T**ake in meaningful chunks
- **E**xpand your field of vision
- **R**elativistic reading

Look back at the progression chart in the Introduction and work out how much your speed has improved. If you think about it, you have only done 12 tests, compared with thousands of readings the 'old' way. Speed reading is therefore still a fragile habit.

This book is only the beginning of your journey to becoming a super speed reader. Do not let yourself lapse into old habits. I suggest that you repeat the relativistic exercise (see Chapter 7) before any extended period of reading. Try to implement the techniques in this book whenever possible in your day-to-day reading. With sustained practice you can continue to progress to almost any speed you desire.

brilliant example

The following graphs show improvements in speed reading on recent courses. When working with a group, all reading tests are only one minute in duration.

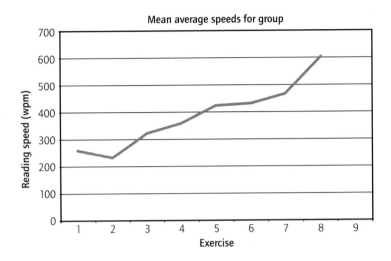

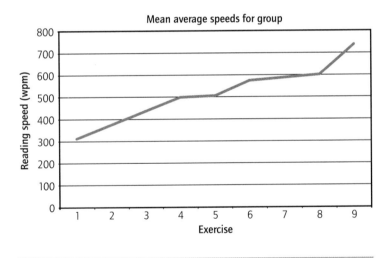

Do you remember our list of statements from Chapter 1 that you identified as true or false? In fact, all the statements are false. Let's consider each of them in turn:

Don't subvocalise (say the words under your breath to yourself or hear the words in your head)

As we saw in Chapter 8, subvocalisation doesn't markedly slow you down and, if used appropriately, can greatly aid both comprehension and recall.

Using your finger to point to words on a page is wrong. It slows you down and is childish

Using your finger or, even better, a slender pointer as a guide for your eyes is very valuable. Contrary to slowing you down, it actually speeds you up! Being 'childlike', rather than 'childish' is a positive thing. As children we correctly and naturally pointed at words.

To understand a book's contents you must read it 'slowly and carefully'

As I have stated many times in this book, reading 'slowly and carefully' is the worst possible advice that a teacher can give. Reading 'rapidly and accurately' would be nearer to the best advice. I am saddened that this is what I was taught at school and annoyed when I see the same myth perpetuated in schools today.

Always start reading at the beginning of a book and go through to the end

This may be good advice if you are reading a detective novel and you don't want to know who the murderer was until the final few pages but for virtually any other type of book, especially study texts, this is bad advice. It is far better to get an overview first, then read the bits that are relevant. It is very rarely that you need to read any book cover to cover, even this one!

Go back and understand what you are reading before you continue reading

This destroys your rhythm and disrupts comprehension. Press onward and you will build more context. It is far easier to see where a jigsaw piece fits when all the pieces around the space are completed. Authors restate the same thing in different ways and elaborate upon a point.

Each word must be read separately

As I explained in Chapters 3, 7 and elsewhere, words should be read in meaningful chunks. This is one of the key speed principles. An added benefit is that these chunks are units of thought so fit together better than disjointed single words, thus making more sense.

As you read faster, your comprehension drops

On the contrary, as you read faster your comprehension increases. Reading slowly gives your mind too much time in between assimilating words so that it can drift, freely associate and wander off the point. If you read quickly there is no time for this to happen so you are more focused and your thoughts more closely follow the author's ideas.

Look up a word that you do not know right away

If you get to the end of a chapter and still don't comprehend what you have read, then add the new words to your vocabulary learning list and look them up, but not before.

It isn't natural to read fast

It isn't 'normal' to read fast but it is absolutely natural. What could be more natural than reading at the speed you think?

You cannot appreciate the material if you read it fast

As I have stated many times, you get a better appreciation of material if you read it fast. If you want to savour the evocative language of a poem and let your imagination roam freely, nobody is going to stop you, but the decision is yours.

Motivation plays no role in reading speed

This is so important to reading that I devoted almost the whole of Chapter 4 to motivation. Your frame of mind is absolutely key to the effectiveness of your reading.

It is not necessary to rest or exercise your eyes

Resting the eyes and changing your focus from time to time is vitally important to maintain healthy vision, prevent excessive tiredness and continue to be able to assimilate the words on a page or screen.

Comprehension should always be 100 per cent

It is very rare that comprehension is 100 per cent, no matter what speed you read at. It is usually unnecessary to have 100 per cent comprehension. You do not remember 100 per cent of what you read and you wouldn't want to. Imagine if someone asked you a question about something that you had read and you had to recite every single word. You comprehend, understand and store the salient details and important points.

You cannot see any wider than a page

The only conceivable way this could be true is if you wore horse's blinkers and held the book directly in front of your nose. As you experienced in the exercise at the end of Chapter 4, your visual field is far wider and higher than a page.

You can only read what you are directly focusing on visually

You can take in a whole page in your peripheral vision and get useful information from it, so your central focus is only part of your brain's reading resources.

You must not mark or write on books

You must not mark or write on library books in ink. You can write on any book in pencil. Highlighting, underlining and writing in the margins improves a book and makes it your own. When I was at university, old textbooks were sold off in the student's union after the exams. There was always demand for the books that had belonged to someone who got a first class degree as they had the best notes in the margins!

? brilliant questions and answers

Q How do I speed read when travelling?

A The best environment for reading is an office or study with a desk, appropriate lighting, decor and seating. However, you may find yourself in situations, such as whilst travelling, where you have time to read but less than ideal conditions. In these instances you have to be pragmatic and sacrifice some of the techniques.

On aeroplanes, especially travelling economy class, if you were to hold your book at almost arm's length you would be hitting the head of the person in the row in front. In this case hold the book as far away as you can in the confines of your seat. Try to maximise the amount of light available, ideally with the window blinds up if travelling in daylight. You can still use a guide, take in groups of words, avoid backskipping and minimise fixation times. Another problem with aircraft is the noisy environment. You can wear earplugs and possibly noise-cancelling headphones on some airlines.

If you travel on trains, try to get a seat with a table. In this case you are able to apply all the techniques as it is almost like sitting at a desk at home. You do need to be mindful of other passengers and not monopolise the whole table but this shouldn't be a problem if the train isn't especially full. If you are forced to have one of the airline style seats you have to follow the guidelines above for planes. One major problem with trains is the vibration that makes it slightly difficult to use a guide effectively. Try your best.

Buses, coaches and tube trains also have the problem of vibration, noise and lack of space. Once again you may have to sacrifice holding the book at the correct distance but will probably be able to use most of the other techniques.

Do not be put off by the odd looks of other passengers or your own self-consciousness. As long as you are not inconveniencing others or getting in their way, any issues they have with your reading techniques are their problem, not yours!

▶

Your comprehension and speed will not be anywhere near your peak but nevertheless you will be better off than reading 'traditionally'.

Q How do I continue to practise once I've finished reading this book?

A The goal of speed reading is to use it in your everyday reading. It is relatively easy to calculate your reading speed. If you are reading Microsoft Word documents you can use the 'word count' function to determine how many words you have read and time yourself. If reading a book, just count the number of words in four or five lines, take the average and then multiply this by the number of lines you read. This will not be absolutely accurate but is good enough to gauge your progress.

Q What do I do if my speed reaches a plateau and I don't seem to be able to progress?

A Keep up your practice. It may take a little while but do not be put off. Make sure that you are applying all the techniques in this book, paying special attention to the procedures for managing your state-of-mind in Chapter 4.

Q What if my speed goes down?

A Whilst your average performance should move upwards there will probably be some instances when you suffer temporary setbacks. This is to be expected. The important thing is how you deal with these. Don't beat yourself up, be despondent or frustrated. 'Failures' are a great opportunity to learn. Analyse what went wrong and try something else.

'Many of life's failures are people who did not realise how close they were to success when they gave up.'

Thomas Edison

Dyslexia

One of the surprising applications of speed reading is to help dyslexics to read more efficiently. This is counterintuitive as you may think that if someone struggles to read in the traditional way, it is fruitless to try to apply a more advanced technique.

According to the British Dyslexia Association, 10 per cent of the British population are dyslexic, 4 per cent severely so. Some studies show that the condition tends to be more prevalent in boys than girls and often runs in families. It has no relationship to IQ and sufferers of dyslexia are generally of average or above average intelligence with more developed artistic abilities. The symptoms of dyslexia can differ from person to person, and each individual with the condition will have a unique pattern of strengths and weaknesses. However, some typical symptoms include:

- *Slow writing speed* – someone may be very knowledgeable about a certain subject but they may have problems expressing that knowledge in writing.
- *Problems with reading fluency* – reading fluency is the ability to read text smoothly, rapidly and automatically, without having to use any, or little, conscious effort. In adulthood this often leads to efforts to conceal difficulties including:
  - trying to avoid reading and writing whenever possible;
  - relying on memory and verbal skills, rather than reading or writing.

Using a guide for reading can significantly help in reading fluency. Moving the guide in a smooth fluid motion allows the eyes to track across the page more smoothly and rapidly.

A related condition, often misdiagnosed as dyslexia as it has similar symptoms, is Irlen Syndrome or Scotopic Sensitivity Syndrome (SSS). This was first identified by educational psychologist Dr Helen Irlen whilst working with adult learners in California in the early 1980s.

SSS is a specific type of perceptual problem that affects the way the brain processes visual information. It is not an optical problem. For those with the condition, the brain is unable to process the full spectrum of light. This results in a range of distortions in perception of the environment and the printed page. These include text that drifts, shifts, shakes, blurs, runs together, disappears or becomes difficult to see. It is often exacerbated by environmental factors such as lighting, brightness, glare, high contrast, patterns and colours.

Reading more rapidly alleviates this problem. The rate of movement or drift of text remains constant whilst reading speed increases. Thus the amount of drift relative to the number of words read decreases. Or put more simply, the words have been read before they've had a chance to go anywhere!

In addition to speed reading, coloured overlays that reduce glare can eliminate the problem. The company Irlen UK also offer tinted lenses customised to block the specific wavelengths of light that affect the sufferer.

Range reading

One very important aspect of speed reading is that this is only one option in a range of reading speeds. It all depends on your needs.

If you have limited time and need the gist of a report then you can skim it at 3,000 words per minute or faster. You won't get a very high level of comprehension but you won't need it.

If you want to study a chapter of a textbook in depth you might read it at 600–800 wpm and then possibly make notes or create a Mind Map.

If you are reading fiction to relax, you may read at anything from 200–400 wpm. You can read fiction much faster, as Anne Jones showed with *Harry Potter*.

If you want to savour a poem, you could read at 100 wpm. Or read it once quickly and once slowly or even several times.

If you take a book to bed with the sole aim of going to sleep, you may read a few pages or even a few paragraphs and fall completely asleep. Your reading speed will be 60 wpm or maybe even slower but it is perfect for the purpose.

Usain Bolt can run 100 metres in 9.58 seconds but I am sure he occasionally likes to take a stroll to the shops! Just because you can read very fast doesn't mean you always have to. It is always your choice.

I hope you have enjoyed reading this book and I wish you brilliant success in your future speed reading.

Appendix 1

Answers to comprehension questions

Introduction

1 False.

2 As 'the aggregation of marginal gains'.

3 Practice (the more you use them the more natural the techniques become).

4 Simply by changing the distance that you hold your book you can improve the efficiency of your vision, reduce eye strain, fatigue and improve both speed and comprehension.

5 Skimming and scanning.

6 Use of a guide, once mastered, is one of the most important techniques in speed reading.

7 The flexibility to alter text to suit your own preferences.

8 Latin and Greek.

Chapter 1

1 $900 billion.

2 Spam filtering and intelligent internet search tools.

3 The average reading speed is in the region of 200 to 240 words per minute (wpm) with about 60 to 80 per cent comprehension.

4 400 words per minute.

5 4,000 words per minute.

6 Any two from: Fear, Overload, Frustration, Guilt and Social Pressure, Lack of Focus, Boredom.

7 Ask yourself questions.

Chapter 2

1 Phonics/Synthetic Phonics and Look-Say.

2 Recognition, Assimilation, Comprehension, Understanding, Storage, Recall, Communicating, Applying and Creating.

3 Any one from: Physical wellbeing, Environment, Emotional state.

Chapter 3

1 Between a quarter and one-and-a-half seconds.

2 Pausing on individual words, skipping backwards and wandering.

3 True.

4 With training, an average person can identify minute images flashed on the screen for only one five-hundredth of a second (2 ms).

5 With practice your eyes can focus on four to six words in a single fixation, depending on length.

6 'Read this passage slowly and carefully'.

7 b) Continue reading.

8 Backskipping and regression account for a 10 to 20 per cent reduction in potential reading speed.

Chapter 4

1 Everything is in some way connected to everything else.

2 Delta (0.5–3 Hz), Theta (4–7 Hz), Alpha (8–12 Hz), Beta (13–25 Hz).

3   The best state for learning is in the Alpha to Theta range.

4   False.

5   Any two from: Listening to baroque music, Anchoring, Visualisation or Audio Visual Entrainment.

6   Imagine something valuable is at stake, consider your goals or think about why you are reading.

Chapter 5

1   We have a wider field of vision horizontally. From an evolutionary point of view, it was important for our hunter-gatherer ancestors to be sensitive to potential predators from either the left or right.

2   Cones support daytime vision and the perception of colour and are more densely packed in the centre of the macula region of the retina in a small pit called the fovea.

3   About 50 cm from your eyes.

4   80 per cent.

5   Comprehension is improved if you have a general idea of the structure of a page; making use of peripheral vision also helps you remember what you read and leads to a reduction of eyestrain, headaches, neck and back pain.

6   True.

Chapter 6

1.   True.

2.   It is believed to control sleep, wakefulness, and the ability to consciously focus attention on something. In addition, the RAS acts as a filter, dampening down the effect of repeated stimuli.

3.   Skimming differs from scanning in the important respect that it is less pre-directed.

4 Skimming is ideal for newspapers.

5 Being selective with your reading can multiply the time saved from reading faster by a factor of four.

6 When reading scientific papers, you generally only need to read the title and abstract.

7 Just read the title to see if it is relevant to continue, skim the contents and if you think it is important, read the executive summary.

Chapter 7

1 Two of the following: adding up a column of figures in your head, scanning classified ads in a newspaper, finding a phone number in a printed directory, looking up a word in a dictionary, reading stock prices in the financial pages of a newspaper.

2 Focus on the page; reduce the duration of fixations; take in groups of words in meaningful chunks; only move forwards and avoid backskipping.

3 Using your finger as a guide has one major disadvantage, that the rest of your hand partially covers the page.

4 A knitting needle, chopstick, pen, pencil or even a conductor's baton.

Chapter 8

1 False.

2 'Of' is what is known as a function word. It does not convey information in itself so the brain glosses over it.

3 If you get to the end of a chapter and really have no clue what the author was saying then it is worth looking up unfamiliar words.

4 80 per cent.

5   We remember approximately 10 per cent of what we read compared with 30 per cent of what we see and up to 90 per cent of what we do.

6   Pay particular attention to graphs, charts and diagrams. Try to imagine pictorial representations or analogies.

7   False.

8   When you read something important turn the volume of subvocalisation right up so you are shouting the words in your head.

Chapter 9

1   Asking questions before you begin enables your subconscious to go to work as soon as you open the book. You will be on the lookout for particular facts and will be more likely to spot relevant information.

2   Most information tends to be concentrated at the beginning and end of chapters.

3   Just jump over them and continue reading.

4   Images promote creativity and imagination. A central image is more interesting, keeps you focused, helps you concentrate, and gives your brain more stimulation.

5   The brain filters out the mundane and ordinary. Exaggeration makes things extraordinary.

6   If you miss a connection the chain breaks and it is very difficult to continue. The Method of Loci lets you carry on even if you miss one or more items in a list.

7   We naturally remember more from the start of a learning session and a reasonable amount from the end.

8   Five.

9   20 minutes (one third).

Chapter 10

1 Set aside a specific time each day devoted to answering important emails.

2 Full spectrum halogen light bulbs that burn brighter, whiter and hotter and are much closer to daylight than other bulbs.

3 Colour combinations that differ widely in luminance.

4 For online reading, sans serif fonts seem easier on the eyes.

5 1.5 spacing.

6 False.

7 50 cm (the same as a page of text).

8 Blinking, stretching and focusing eyes on distant objects.

9 Approximately every 15 to 20 minutes.

Chapter 11

1 Neophilia – a tendency to like anything new; love of novelty.

2 Spheroid – shaped like, but not exactly, a sphere.

3 Geochronologist – one who studies the ordering and dating of events in the earth's history, including the origin of the earth itself.

4 Polycyclic – having more than one cyclic component.

5 Controvertible – capable of being disputed as true or opposed by reasoning.

6 Heptad – a group or series of seven.

7 Whitherward – in what direction.

8 Semicentennial – A fiftieth anniversary or its celebration.

9 Polyphony – having many tones or voices; a style of musical composition employing two or more simultaneous but relatively independent melodic lines.

10 Chronophobia – fear of time.

Appendix 2

Speed reading hall of fame

The table below shows the top 20 results from official speed reading competitions conducted at the Mind Sports Olympiad between 1998 and 2005. 'Effective speed' is calculated by multiplying speed by percentage comprehension. Competitors are tested on unpublished novels.

Ranking	First name	Surname	Year	Judge	Country	Gross wpm	Compre-hension	Effective wpm
1	Anne	Jones	2001	MSO	England	2,246	60%	1,348
2	Alexander	Baron	1999	MSO	England	2,192	40%	877
3	Benjamin	Crowne	2001	MSO	England	1,438	60%	863
4	Kenneth	Wilshire	1999	MSO	Wales	2,140	38%	803
5	Bethan	Ruddock	2005	MSO	England	955	80%	764
6	Adel	Anwar	1999	MSO	England	3,289	23%	740
7	Pablo	Rivera	1999	MSO	Puerto Rico	3,289	23%	740
8	Roberto	Alfanador	1999	MSO	America	3,614	20%	723
9	Ricardo	Cordero	1999	MSO	Puerto Rico	3,614	20%	723
10	Andrew	Harvey	2004	MSO	England	918	72%	661
11	Daniel	Bradbury	2004	MSO	England	1,006	62%	623
12	Henry	Hopking	2003	MSO	England	1,330	46%	610
13	Nathalie	Lecordier	2001	MSO	England	1,231	40%	492
14	Demetris	Pillas	2001	MSO	Cyprus	2,037	24%	489
15	Lana	Israel	1998	MSO	USA	?	?	461
16	Charles	Cutbush	2004	MSO	Australia	1,080	40%	432
17	George	Lane	2004	MSO	England	528	72%	380
18	Judith	Bradbury	2005	MSO	England	806	42%	336
19	Milagros	Castro	1999	MSO	America	4,478	8%	336
20	Daniel	Holloway	1999	MSO	England	1,463	23%	329

Further reading

Buzan, Tony, *Buzan's Study Skills*, BBC Active, Pearson, Harlow, 2011.

Buzan, Tony, *The Speed Reading Book*, BBC Active, Pearson, Harlow, 2010.

Buzan, Tony, *The Power of Verbal Intelligence*, Thorsons, London, 2002.

Buzan, Tony and Buzan, Barry, *The Mind Map Book*, BBC Active, Pearson, Harlow, 2010.

Chambers, Phil and Colliar, Elaine, *A Mind to do Business*, ECPC Publications, Bucknell, 2004.

Chambers, Phil and Colliar, Elaine, *The Student Survival Guide*, 2nd edition, ECPC Publications, Bucknell, 2008.

Chambers, Phil, *101 Top Tips for Better Mind Maps*, ECPC Publications, Bucknell, 2005.

Dale, Edgar, *Audiovisual Methods in Teaching*, Dryden Press, NY, 1969.

Ebbinghaus, Hermann, *A Contribution to Experimental Psychology*, translated by H.A. Ruger and C.E. Bussenius, 1913, Columbia University, NY, 1885 (see **http://psychclas sics.yorku.ca/Ebbinghaus/index.htm**).

Greenfield, Susan, *Tomorrow's People*, Penguin, London, 2004.

Griffiths, Chris with Costi, Melina, *Grasp The Solution*, Proactive Press, Cardiff, 2011.

O'Brien, Dominic, *You Can Have an Amazing Memory*, Watkins Publishing, London, 2011.

Rauscher, F.H., Shaw, GL. and Ky, K.N., 'Music and Spatial Task Performance', *Nature*, 1993, 365: 611.

Segall, M.H., Campbell, D.T. and Herskovits, M.J., *The Influence of Culture on Visual Perception*, Bobbs-Merrill, Oxford, 1966.

Useful websites

http://colorusage.arc.nasa.gov/luminance_cont.php

www.bdadyslexia.org.uk

www.learning-tech.co.uk

www.thinkbuzan.com

www.peakperformancetraining.org (Dominic O'Brien)

Index